WOMEN AND GARDENS

ALSO BY THE AUTHORS

BOOKS BY JUDITH MUNDLAK TAYLOR

The Olive in California: history of an immigrant tree (2000)

Tangible Memories: Californians and their gardens 1800-1950 (2003)

The Global Migrations of Ornamental Plants: how the world got into your garden (2009)

Visions of Loveliness: the work of forgotten flower breeders (2014)

An Abundance of Flowers: more great flower breeders of the past (2018)

A Five Year Plan for Geraniums: growing flowers commercially in East Germany 1946-1989 (2019)

BOOKS BY SUSAN GROAG BELL (1926–2015)

Women, from the Greeks to the French Revolution (1973, reprinted 1980)

Women, the Family, and Freedom: The Debate in the Documents, 1750-1950 (1983), with Karen Offen

Between Worlds: Czechoslovakia, England, and America (1991)

The Lost Tapestries of the City of Ladies (2004)

For Ellen

WOMEN AND GARDENS

OBSTACLES AND OPPORTUNITIES FOR WOMEN GARDENERS THROUGHOUT HISTORY

Judith

JUDITH MUNDLAK TAYLOR
AND THE LATE SUSAN GROAG BELL

TAYLORHORT PRESS

Cover illustration: *Celia Thaxter's Garden, Isle of Shoals, Maine* (1890), by Childe Hassam; used with permission from The Metropolitan Museum of Art. Image source Art Resource, New York, NY.

Frontispiece: Women gardeners at Kew, circa 1915
© Board of Trustees the Royal Botanic Gardens, Kew, London, England.

Text copyright © 2021 by Judith Mundlak Taylor

Published by TaylorHort Press
San Francisco, CA

www.horthistoria.com
judith@horthistoria.com

ISBN: 978-0-578-94247-6

Library of Congress Control Number: 2021912452

CONTENTS

WOMEN AND GARDENS

INTRODUCTION

This book celebrates the achievements of women in gardening and horticulture. They have come a very long way in the last hundred and fifty years, with the pace accelerating in the more recent past. At present there are more women in landscape architecture than men. It was not always so. The authors trace that path over several centuries, uncovering the gardening work of women. Official history has been written by men for millennia. This has usually been left unsaid but is part of the dictum: "history is written by the victors." Historians saw no need to include anything about women and their contributions. Women and their doings were of no moment to them. They did not see them as fully adult.

During her long and distinguished career, the late Susan Groag Bell (1926–2015) published several seminal works on women's place in history and how it had largely been written out. In her 1982 article "Medieval Women Book Owners: Arbiters of Lay Piety and Ambassadors of Culture" in the journal *Signs,* she argued that noblewomen in medieval society, remaining folded within their clearly delineated roles, still affected society by educating their children through books.[81] They commissioned new ones and argued with the authors to offer devotional works in vernacular languages, not only Latin. When their daughters married and moved to a new household, they carried all this with them. Women acted as agents in the transfer of civilization working almost invisibly.

Bell's article became widely influential and inspired other scholars to analyze how women were obscured in historical records. Pointing out how women had very little opportunity to lead public lives, she drew attention to injustices in historiography.

At her death, an outline for a book about women and gardens was found in her papers, going back to 1976. It was divided into eight chapters with an optional ninth one. The first four chapters illuminated Susan Bell's thoughts about women and gardens in art and literature, largely intangible matters, what I (JMT) am defining as "passive." She then changed over to much more pragmatic questions about actual women and actual gardens on the ground, "active." This set her thinking about the impediments to women owning, designing, and working in gardens in the past few hundred years. She moved from the vaguely general view to highly specific examples.

This switch seemed to me (JMT) to be more in keeping with her primary goal of women taking their rightful places in society. She herself had suffered from the disability of being a woman in her professional life. In order to bring this unfinished work to the public, I have taken the liberty of editing her material and adding my own perspectives, based on her work, in order to examine the history of the obstacles and opportunities for women in gardens.

Why is it necessary to write a book about the history of women and gardens? For one thing, Bell found that her colleagues fell about laughing when she suggested that this could be a fruitful source of academic enquiry. Such a response from people who should have known better is one very good reason to look into the matter further. The encouraging news is that since her aperçu in the late 1970s, a number of excellent books on the topic have been published, both in the United States and the United Kingdom.

References to women and women's contribution to horticulture were previously few and far between. This, as we know from the general study of women's history, means little because women's contribution has typically been taken for granted, ignored, or simply not recorded as being so obvious. It happens constantly, even now, at a time when historians should be aware of the open questions on women's history in many areas.

The facts are not in doubt. Women have always gardened, either for survival or pleasure. Even during the periods when it was not comme il faut for ladies to garden, there are many records of them doing just that. The interest lies in the fact that this was another front in the never-ending fight for recognition that women were serious adults, capable of becoming professional gardeners or in fact anything they chose. It was not until late in the nineteenth century that they started taking part in landscape gardening and other professions normally the province of men: i.e., their activity shifted from purely local and personal to the possibility of being public and professional.

There is a supposed affinity between women and gardens but its interpretation for a certain set of women has changed over time, from passive and decorative to healthily active. This affinity is not an incontrovertible fact but emerged as the result of cumulative observation. It became a plausible peg on which to hang all manner of ideas. No doubt the connection may be unconscious but both women and the land are fecund and the source of new life. Women are said to be nurturing by nature. It is incontrovertible that gardens require nurturing, but half a century of modern gender studies have taught us to question all these other assumptions.

Perhaps the most important impetus to women becoming professional gardeners was the effort to obtain the vote. All the crucial changes which are considered in this book took place in the same era as that monumental struggle, the second half of the nineteenth century and the early years of the twentieth century. The right for women over thirty to vote was finally acknowledged in 1918 in the United Kingdom. Canadian women were allowed to vote in 1918. In the United States an act to permit women to vote was passed in 1920. Without being openly stated this pertained solely to white women. All women were allowed to vote in the United Kingdom in 1928.

The struggle was led by strong women with broad vision. They did not have gardening in their minds, but the fact that women banded together to share ideas helped to set the scene. Previously women only got together to do charity work, such as sewing circles or visiting the poor, very worthy aims. These informal gatherings nevertheless provided a basis on which they could work together for other purposes.

Women were in the forefront of abolishing slavery. Nursing was made into a profession by Florence Nightingale, though she worked alone using men as her mouthpieces. Planning strategy to obtain the vote was another step in their social development.

The purpose of this book is to look into the obstacles and opportunities for women in gardening, not just whether they were able to till the soil themselves. That is a given. Susan Bell adduced a great deal of evidence about women happily gardening in the centuries they were supposedly not doing it, as now have other authors.

Women and gardens form a broad generalization which needs to be clarified. Which women? When one thinks about friends and relatives, only some of the women are committed gardeners. A great many are not the slightest bit interested. For those who are, the range is from fanatics in sturdy old clothes with dirt under their fingernails to urban dilettantes tending a few square feet of grass and some potted plants. Which gardens? A few culinary herbs on a kitchen window sill can qualify as a garden.

The connection with gardens can become a metaphor for the condition of women and attitudes toward them even now. It can be a symbol of women's exclusion from meaningful occupations previously populated only by men. The signal to noise ratio in this investigation is not sharply defined. The background noise has to be firmly silenced to tease out the answers.

What do I mean by "background noise?" It is the fact that most agricultural and garden work has been done by nameless and faceless women over the millennia and still is in many places. Those women do not have the luxury of choice: plant rice, grow vegetables, or starve. A book like this looks at the motivation and goals of women who do not require that level of drudgery simply to stay alive but yet voluntarily undertake the hard physical labor needed for gardening, i.e. women of leisure and means. Even then questions arise about which epoch is being considered.

Susan Bell set out to examine the representation of women and gardens in art and literature, then turned to their actual participation in gardening work. Representative art was used to illuminate religious practice such as in breviaries or the Book of Hours. It also reflected the dual roles of woman in men's eyes as either the temptress Eve or the pristine Virgin Mary. The Biblical Eve's original sin took place in the Garden of Eden.

The scope of this book is confined to Western cultures, largely derived from Northern European origins, over about the last five hundred years. Women work in and with gardens all over the world but Susan Bell did not attempt to make her survey global. It is very interesting to think briefly about how and why such gardening work might differ, both because of climate factors and cultural attitudes. Even in a survey only covering the European and Anglophone groups, wide variations in climate still dictate garden activity.

The southern states of the United States are semitropical. The warm, even tropical countries of Central and South America in the modern era were initially founded by Iberian settlers whose attitudes to manual labor as well as to women also differed. The first Spanish men who arrived in what is now Mexico City commented on the flourishing flower and vegetable gardens on pontoons in the lake, run by Aztec women. These are all fruitful topics for further research.

Simply sticking to the Northern European and Western tradition, views about women and gardens have fluctuated between extremes. At one pole there was the grinding necessity of survival by growing plants for food and medicine in which women were simply obscure laborers. At the other pole, a more romanticized view of them as passive adornments to gardens prevailed from the Medieval period on. A few centuries later, some bumptious women set out to create a third variation, women of leisure and means who yet wished to do hard physical labor in gardens.

This difference between the passive and active roles inherently denotes class divisions. That observation informed Susan Bell's study. Very poor women always slaved actively in fields and gardens throughout history and no one thought anything of it. Babies were slung on their backs or watched by an older sibling. A small number of women from that class managed to obtain a little respect by understanding the therapeutic properties of some wild plants, giving them a modicum of recognition and status in the village. This work was considered to be solely a women's province but if they did it too well they could be accused of dealing in the dark arts and tried as witches.

To show how that this is a cultural assumption, consider the work of shamans in many societies, including some of the indigenous populations of the Southwestern United States. The therapeutic rituals include drugs derived from wild plants around them. Shamans are always male. Women had best not go there.

Starting at about the earliest epoch of modern Western mores, the role of the chatelaine in a Norman castle was intermediate between the active and passive. Such a woman was not expected to get her hands dirty but she was required to know a great deal about the preservation of food and the use of herbal drugs, also known as "simples," while supervising the work of her servants. If she neglected this duty, the people in the castle might starve in the winter. The products of the woods, fields, and garden formed the basis of her skill but at one remove. It was still a passive role for an upper-class woman. She learned this lore from her mother, grandmother and other older women around her.

Women's literacy was a byproduct of managing a large household. There is an assumption that women were not taught to read in the medieval period but some of the earliest books ever printed were herbal and housewifely guides for aristocratic housekeepers. There is evidence in England that girls and women, taught by religious sisters, were reading perfectly well before the Norman conquest but that the Normans did not bother about it. High born men of the time did not read either. Why should they? They had clerks who could do it for them. Religion was the other stimulus for women's literacy but the lavish illustrations in a breviary obviated the need to be able to read well.

Staying in our Norman castle, shifting from the intermediate to the passive mode, the lady of the house might relax, sitting under a bower on a turf bench in the tiny rooftop garden on the keep. Red and white roses grew around her and the lawn was dotted with daffodils ("asphodels"), violets and pinks. I for one would not be too keen to sit on a damp turf bench but it looked very decorative.

Activity and passivity provide a framework for Bell's study but at what point did the active largely replace the passive? The crux of Susan Bell's work is the cognitive dissonance caused by comfortably off women wishing to do manual labor in a garden and the forces that stopped them. Her narrative moves in that direction, largely omitting the unsung peasant, not because of social bias but because she did not find much to tell.

Her chapter headings included women's joy in garden work and its beneficial effect on their health, women as professional gardeners, women as designers and architects of gardens, women as teachers of horticulture, as breeders of new flowers and even women as market gardeners. In other words, women took on the entire gamut of gardening so that currently many people regard gardening as the true occupation of women, even if some of them are just there for the garden club in a flowery hat and frilly dress.

Approached in this way, it is clear that Susan Bell was actually writing two books in one. The first half examined the passive roles of wealthy women but the second half moved into the active ones, quite a different story. Women were popping up where they were not supposed to be, disrupting society. If anyone remembers the delightful Horn and Hardart Automats, they are an analogy for what was happening. The customer put his or her coin into a slot and then opened the little hatch containing whichever dish he or she had chosen. To get a different dish you only had to put a coin in another slot and repeat the process. Imagine the consternation when the customer chose fried chicken and the hatch revealed apple pie. Women were safely ensconced behind specific hatches.

As Samuel Johnson remarked to Boswell about women preachers, "Sir, a woman's preaching is like a dog's walking on his hind legs. It is not done well; but you are surprised to find it done at all." [84] Boswell had heard a woman preach at a Quaker service that morning, perhaps a woman like Ann Hutchinson, who was exiled to America for so egregiously breaking the rules. The Hutchinson River in New York is named for her. Women were getting into matters which were not their province and trying to overcome social expectations. Dr. Johnson valued Mrs. Thrale's intellect but could not imagine her doing anything more than chatter over tea.

I would like to explore the way in which the leisured women finally separated themselves from being a faceless mass of simpering misses with muzzy bird brains good only for reproduction and became individual actors capable of contributing to previously solely masculine fields. What were their obstacles and opportunities? Not all women were capable of accomplishing this but then neither can all men. Intelligence and a capacity for sustained application range along bell-shaped curves for both sexes. Being a man did not automatically qualify you to be a fine gardener, a breeder of new flowers or a designer of landscapes but why should being a woman have automatically disqualified you from trying?

. . .

This achievement in gardening is not the end of the story for women to be whole people but it does level the playing field a little. Successful businesswomen still find themselves being condescended to, sent to get coffee, addressed as "honey" and told to take notes at meetings.

The journey toward acceptance has taken about 150 years but women now routinely inhabit the horticultural sphere. That has happened simultaneously with them adopting the professions of medicine, law, politics, science, religion, engineering and pretty well any other one they so choose.

Judith Mundlak Taylor
San Francisco, California
October 2020

1

OBSTACLES

MALE ENCROACHMENT INTO FIELDS
PREVIOUSLY MANAGED BY WOMEN

Women wanted to work in fields previously denied to them.
It is somewhat ironic that this usurpation worked both ways.
The overtaking of masculine professions, in the present case
horticulture, by women anxious to make proper use of their
talents, is what is at issue here. Before launching into that
recital, it is important to understand that women also gave
up something along the line. In addition to managing their
households, treating the inevitable minor ailments everyone
encounters at one time or another had been the unique
province of women over the centuries. They were the family
doctors. This function was at stake.

Women played the same role not only in the parent
European countries but in the colonies which they spun off
in the New World. Such women used a variety of methods
to heal and cure, the most important of which were

"simples," drugs derived from plants initially found growing wild but later planted intentionally in gardens. In the antebellum South the mistress of the plantation was often the only "doctor" a slave would know. Piety and charity played a role but there was also the reality that slaves were valuable property and thus needed maintenance.

From Saxon and Norman times even a small cottage had a sliver of land around it, known as the "curtilage." Its upkeep was considered to be the responsibility of the woman in the house. In it she would plant her indispensable herbs and flowers. Many flowers had dual roles, not only beauty but medicinal powers. As mentioned elsewhere in this book, *Digitalis purpurea*, foxglove, was handsome but also had highly therapeutic leaves. Roses served three functions: beauty, fragrance and nutrition. Rose petals were strewn on a bed or the floor to give off their scent. The hips were crushed and preserved in syrup for the winter. It is now known that rose hips have a greater concentration of vitamin C, ascorbic acid, than many other fruits, including oranges.

Susan Groag Bell was interested both in the development of women's contribution to gardening in western civilization and in the psychological reasons for women's keen horticultural activity, which she saw as a creative and emotional refuge. She apologized for her occasionally impressionistic style, writing with the hope that some of her readers who were interested in specific areas or periods would be inspired to help her fill the historical gaps, both geographically and quantitatively.

16th century English writers on husbandry were very specific about the fact that the garden was woman's preserve. Since these writers took this so clearly for granted, and moreover rural traditions change so very slowly, we may perhaps be permitted to ascribe the same effort to women in earlier centuries, from which we have only occasional hints of women's gardening.

For example, Fitzherbert in his famous *A new trace or treatise most profytable for All Husbandmen* (1523) wrote: "And in the begynninge of Marche, or a lyttell afore, is tyme for a wyfe to make her garden, and to gette as many good sedes and herbes as she canne, and specially suche as be good for the potte and to eate and as ofte as nede shall requyre it must be weded, for else the wedes wyl overgrow the herbes."[54]

Thomas Tusser, whose *100 Pointes of Goode Husbandrie* (1557) went into approximately twenty-eight editions, had no doubt about gardening being woman's work.[55] He wrote: "In March, April, and May from morning to night in sowing and setting good huswives delight To have in a garden, or other like plot, to turn up their house, and to furnish their pot," or "Wife into thy garden and set me a plot with strawberry rootes of the best to be got," and, "Good Huswifes in somer will save their own seedes against the next year, as occasion needes. One seede for another, to make exchange, with fellowlie neighbourhood seemeth not strange." Perhaps John Langland's Bett the Alewife, who carried peony seeds, garlic, and fennel seed in her bag was about to make such a neighbourly exchange in the 1370s.

The Menagier of Paris, Fitzherbert, and Tusser wrote about women who actually tended their own garden with its mixture of vegetable, herb, and flower — a mixture of utility and delight. Some women hired themselves out as day labourers like Joan Perry, or Margaret Hall, or the women "rooting up unprofitable herbs" in the garden of Christchurch College at Oxford in 1530, or the "weeder women" kept in the garden and orchard at Hampton Court. Others, like "Griselda" in Chaucer's *Clerks' Tale,* would gather "Roots, herbs and other grasses" on their way home and use them to flavor their cooking. Still others were in the florists' business. The Menagier of Paris decreed that "a woman chaplet-maker should deliver garlands on the wedding eve and wedding day."

From all of this, we have some picture of the medieval woman gardener, whether she did indeed supervise a castle garden, work the curtilage surrounding her cottage or gathered wildflowers and herbs for garlands or cooking pot. The picture can be confirmed with illuminations in books and woodcuts from the fifteenth and sixteenth centuries.

If we peruse the herbals of the early periods or even modern works like *Herbs and Other Medicinal Plants,* or John Lust's *The Herb Book,* it becomes clear that almost every wild plant, however common or however rare, had a variety of culinary and medicinal uses that were the basis of cookery and of the physicians' remedies till well into the 18th and 19th centuries. [62, 63] Women were both the cooks and the family physicians. Until the 16th century, only women were expected to concern themselves with the medical problems of pregnancy, childbirth and its aftermath. Housewives, midwives, and nurses had to have some knowledge of the medicinal properties of plants and would, one would think, be more knowledgeable if they themselves understood the growth process, soil, and the climatic conditions that were pertinent to specific plants.

One folk belief that persisted for centuries was heeding the ideal time to plant. Some seeds did best if put into the ground by the light of the full moon, or so it was said. Thomas Tusser wrote of "good huswifes" providing "cold herbes in hir garden for agues that balm" and "rose water and treakle to comfort the heart."[55] Nursing mothers' and children's problems are treated equally with large varieties of herbal mixtures. The severe cough of a baby can be cured by a draught of hyssop and wild thyme cooked in wine; painful eyes can be cured by a fomentation of mallow, violet leaves, bramble tops, and mountain brook willow in the afternoon. A deodorant consisting of a cloth soaked in wine in which leaves and shoots of myrtle have been boiled is recommended for those who have "foul smelling sweat beyond all reason."

Hildegard of Bingen, 1098–1179, the famous twelfth century German abbess, wrote books on philosophy, botany and human reproduction with a knowledge remarkable for one who was had been a nun and in the cloister since the age of seven. Her book, *Causes and Cures*, is concerned with plants and their therapeutic characteristics.[66] It mixes the fantastic with practical good sense. Her recipe for the common cold, for example, calls for one pint of fennel and four pints of dill to be soaked on a roofing tile and the smoke of this mixture to be inhaled through the mouth and nose.

Early remedies using herbs and the recipes handed down orally from Aristotle and Galen and even from rare treatises like Trotula's *Diseases of Women* or Hildegard's *Causes and Cures*, form a fascinating topic but touch only peripherally on the subject of women and gardening.[65] From the 16th century onwards, the "Physic Garden" connected to hospitals and medical schools became a common feature. These gardens were important as sources of plant identification for physicians and apothecaries, now solely male professionals attending universities and schools which excluded women students.

Previously, it is interesting to note, such specialized physic gardens were by no means common. More or less every garden had been a type of physic garden in that it provided the domestic "physician" with her raw material. Now, cures for diseases and herbal lore were to be left to the physicians trained in the new and vigorous male medical schools. It is no surprise that at this time of developing male professionalism, there should have been the greatest witch-hunt in Western Europe, a witch-hunt aimed largely against women (often older, solitary widows) whose experience with herbs and midwifery made them dangerous rivals for the emerging men.

After the 16th century in Europe, ladies of the upper classes, that is, the nobility and the merchant and professional classes, gradually lost their keen practical first-hand involvement with growing and using plants. The garden ceased to be a combination of useful plants whose beauty the woman gardener appreciated as a bonus. Instead, from the 16th century on, it became an ornament, a place for pleasurable relaxation, inspired by Renaissance architects and seekers after ancient Greco-Roman examples.

The shift in emphasis from women as gardeners and physicians to men coincided with the growth of knowledge, stimulated by the discovery of classical learning. With very few exceptions this was limited to men. It is true that Queen Elizabeth I was very well educated as was Sir Thomas More's daughter Margaret but they were very uncommon women. More's second wife Alice stubbornly refused to learn even to read.

The survival of Hadrian's villa from the second century CE and its rediscovery in 1461 inspired a whole new way of creating gardens in Italy and then in other countries. At the peak of the Roman empire, the nobles looked back at Egyptian and Greek styles and used some of them in their architecture. This type of garden's most significant feature was a focus on the what is now called "hardscape:" walls, rooms, grottos, statuary, and water. One might say it was just more of the main house without the weathertight enclosure. It was for dining, plotting, celebrating, relaxation and dalliance in the relevant season. Plants were an afterthought but still played an important role in scenting the air and creating shady arbors.

The Italian Renaissance gardens, architecturally designed and based on the Roman style, became a place where ladies were expected to discuss the philosophy of Platonic love and poetry, to view masques and join in fetes. They might also read elevating, or even not so elevating, books like Boccaccio's *Book of Illustrious Women* or his *Decameron*. [82, 83]

Renaissance queens and ladies of high nobility were as interested in developing fashionable gardens as they were in the New Learning and art generally. They established the tradition of high born ladies being patrons of gardens, causing them to be created without necessarily doing any hard digging themselves. Garden historians note that Elizabeth I was fond of flowers. She had sumptuous gardens laid out at one of her favorite residences: Nonesuch Palace.

. . .

Isabella d'Este's gardens at Porto, near Mantua, were not only in the great new Renaissance style with fountains, statues and reliefs designed by the most exciting new sculptors but they were the background for the development of one of the most famous Renaissance pieces of philosophical literature: *The Courtier.*[91] Castiglione, Elizabetta Gonzaga, and Emilia Pia all enjoyed the shade, "perpetual verdure, luscious fruits and sweetest flowers" of Isabella's gardens at Porto.

Isabella was born in Ferrara in 1474 and married the Marchese Francisco Gonzaga to become the Marchesa of Mantua. Isabella d'Este treasured her gardener as she did her other artists and one of her special kindnesses was to lend him to an old humanist friend whose own garden was sorely neglected.

One of her descendants was Cardinal Ippolito d'Este. He created a splendid garden just near Rome, Villa d'Este. Some of its wonders were the fountains. Fountains were central to Renaissance gardens and often used with a gentle malice to drench the unsuspecting guest if he or she happened to step on a hidden mechanism. If there were no natural torrent nearby flowing downhill, the creators would build aqueducts to transmit the water from far away.

A garden was the one great addition made by Catherine de Medici to the Chateau at Chenonceau. Henri II had installed his mistress, Diane de Poitiers, in the chateau. She created a glorious formal garden. Once Henri died, Catherine lost no time in evicting her rival. To make it clear who was boss, Catherine caused her gardeners to build a second, very similar garden on the other side of the frontage. Chenonceau, which thus now had two French Renaissance gardens, is unique in this respect.

The change from the useful but sweetly scented and peaceful herb, fruit, and vegetable garden of the middle ages became even more dramatic when the sculpture-filled, romantic Italian Renaissance garden was replaced by the strictly formal, almost regimented French designs that developed simultaneously with the military grandeur of Louis XIV's monarchy. The gardens of Versailles, designed by Louis' landscape architect M. Andre Le Notre, became the model of all European courts and small country estates. Queen Henrietta Maria, wife of Charles II, for example, retained Le Notre to reconstruct her garden at the Queen's House, Greenwich when she returned to England after her exile at the French Court during the interregnum.

Louis XIV wanted a vast uniformed aristocracy to surround his person at Versailles, making the upkeep of their own country estates a difficult problem for the gentlemen and ladies of the Court. Louis liked to have his potential rivals right in front of him, not far away fomenting trouble. He acted on the principle of "keep your friends close, your enemies closer." Aristocratic French women very quickly lost touch with hands-on gardening in this sort of existence.

The gardens at Versailles hardly lend themselves to peaceful domestic pursuits. They are more suited to compulsory walks for a bored and physically stiff society. The dense shrubbery did provide a haven for intrigue, both amorous and otherwise. Count Axel von Fersen found it useful for assignations with Marie Antoinette many years later. Such gardens are certainly not a place where a woman might decide to do a little digging in order to calm her emotions or to experiment with a new vegetable. Marie Antoinette knew exactly what she was about when she insisted on having a simple farm and gardens built for her own private pleasure. Vegetables and fruits were now strictly relegated to a special area known as a "potager" or kitchen garden. The garden for ladies became purely ornamental.

The division between utility and ornament paralleled the division between classes from a time when women were in charge of the useful as well as the ornamental. Now, only the passive aspects of the ornamental seemed to be within their domain. In 1577, Barnaby Googe had already looked back nostalgically to the time when, as he wrote, "Herein were the olde husbandes very careful and used always to judge that where they founde the Garden out of order, the wyfe of the house (for unto her belonged the charge thereof) was no good huswyfe."[55]

By 1707, Charles Evelyn, (brother of John) saw gardening as a pleasure, not a necessity, for ladies. In *The Lady's Recreation* (1707) he described carefully how to lay out ornamental flowers, as well as planting orange trees and placing statues, grass plots, and borders. He did not find it necessary to give directions for growing the commonest flowers, such as foxgloves, garden mallows, scabious, fennel, and double lady's smock. "For these," he said, "every Country Dame has in her garden and knows how to sow, plant, and propagate."[13]

Celia Fiennes described approximately thirty gardens of great variety seen during her horseback travels around England in the 1690s.[15] She was impressed by the fashionable garden design incorporating Baroque statues, fountains, and elegant walks, and was able occasionally to compare and describe the plants indicating the sort of knowledgeability referred to by Charles Evelyn. One of the statues she saw indicates that women of the lower classes continued to earn their living as gardeners. Here is Celia Fiennes' description of the garden of the Duke of Bedford at Woburn: "The gardens are fine, there is a large bowling green with 8 arbours kept cut neatley, and seates in each, there is a seate up in a high tree that ascends from the green 50 steps, that commands the whole parke round to see the deer hunted, as also a large prospect of the country."[15]

When early Englishwomen started to migrate to North America in the sixteenth and seventeenth centuries, they made sure to take seeds and cuttings of these plants with them. That tided them over until they began to learn about the plants in their new home, both by their own exploration and listening to advice from the indigenous people.

Then something strange happened. By about the fifteenth century, European women were starting to be systematically shut out of the fields they had previously dominated. Men began a process of displacing women almost by stealth. Women had to cede their one bastion of professional skill, a version of medicine, just because they were women. It was one more step in maintaining the dominance of men. If only men could bear children, they would be completely free of these pesky nuisances.

This all took place slowly enough and over a long enough period of time that no one paid very much attention to what was going on until it was too late. Women worked very locally, in the family and the village. They had no societies or organizations across these boundaries. Women seldom if ever left their neighborhoods to travel and study the way men did. Reducing their influence and effectiveness was all too simple, with no one watching or taking up their cause. One lone voice is easily silenced.

The scientific observations made by inspired men such as Roger Bacon, Galileo, Robert Boyle, and Johannes Kepler, as well as the discovery of Arab science and the Renaissance in general, ushered in a whole new way of doing things based on observed fact rather than religion, tradition, or intuition. These striking intellectual advances were restricted to men. Women were carefully kept in check by serial pregnancies and being perpetually tired because of raising the resulting children. Even if they thought about the movements of the stars or the properties of matter, they had no way of going into those ideas any more deeply.

Throughout history, important male doctors such as Hippocrates and Galen were part of an established tradition. If any women participated at all, it was as assistants. Surgeons like Vesalius learned anatomy on the battle fields in repairing wounds. Willis discovered the circulation of the blood, Antony van Leeuwenhoek found spermatozoa under his little monocular microscope and Joseph Lister developed antiseptic surgery, all a huge march forward in lifesaving medicine entirely done by men.

Perhaps the most significant development in the traditionally female field of obstetrics was made by Ignaz Semelweiss, 1818–1865, at the Allgemeine Krankenhaus in Vienna. He recognized that puerperal sepsis was spread by something from cadavers on the doctor's hands and could be eradicated by washing the hands in a solution of chlorinated lime when entering the maternity ward. (Puerperal sepsis is a devastating infection of the female genital tract after parturition.)

By getting doctors to wash their hands at the door of the obstetric ward, women no longer had to die in childbirth. The American neurosurgeon Harvey Cushing had not yet invented rubber gloves. Semelweiss was working from clinical observation. It would be years before Louis Pasteur discovered bacteria and Robert Koch showed their role in causing disease. His ideas did not make Semelweiss popular. The other doctors were outraged at being told what to do and did everything they could to discredit him. They did not have his penetrating intellect and capacity to make connections and thought it was all nonsense. They were very aggrieved at him. In his efforts to save women, he himself suffered much obloquy and humiliation.

Even when women managed to survive these biological hazards, at the other end of the hospital Sigmund Freud was busily putting them back into their passive gender and sexual boxes. "Hysteria," supposedly a female condition due to the uterus wandering around in the body, covered a multitude of disorders which no one could be bothered to identify. Freud's sexual theories simply locked that all more firmly in place.

CONTRIBUTION OF WOMEN TO MAINSTREAM MEDICAL SCIENCE

Country women continued to take care of sick people but there was a slow trend toward professionally trained men usurping this role. Two very important medical discoveries were ascribed to male physicians but were based on the observations of dairymaids and old "wise women." The first was smallpox, a scourge which killed at least 40% of its victims. The treatment of smallpox was very ineffectual.

Trying to prevent it was the only really helpful approach. There were two important steps in the story of its eradication, one introduced by a woman.

In 1714, Lady Mary Wortley Montagu (1689–1762) lived in Constantinople with her husband, the English minister to the Porte. Lady Mary did not allow herself to be bound by trifling social convention and visited many Turkish women. She noticed their smooth complexions without the ravages of smallpox. She had had an attack of the disease and lost a brother to it. The Turkish ladies explained the practice of "variolation" to her, inoculating a healthy person with a tiny bit of the matter from a smallpox lesion. This protected most of the recipients but not all. A few recipients unfortunately caught the disease itself from the inoculation. *Variolus major* is the technical name of smallpox. (One might reasonably ask if this deadly disease were the "small" pox, what was the great pox? The answer is syphilis.)

Lady Mary saw the potential for better health. She had her children variolated. None of them caught smallpox. When she returned to London, she campaigned to have this practice widely adopted. Variolation was an advance in medical knowledge but not really satisfactory and certainly not part of the academic sphere. Work by the Reverend Cotton Mather, who reportedly learned the method from a slave and Dr. Zabdiel Boylston in the 1721 Boston smallpox epidemic showed that smallpox could be largely controlled by variolation. This was at roughly the same time as Lady Mary was expounding its benefits in England.

The most important figure in the conquest of smallpox was Edward Jenner (1749–1823). He practiced medicine in the Gloucestershire countryside but was no bumbling country practitioner. Jenner had received the best medical education available at the time and was known for other important contributions to medicine. He noticed that dairy maids in constant contact with cows were immune to smallpox. They would say, "I cannot take (catch) the small pox because I have had the cowpox." Jenner knew that cows were susceptible to a disease very much like smallpox called "cowpox" but much milder. Neither the cows nor the dairymaids who caught the infection from them died, nor did the women ever get smallpox.

Jenner was not the first person to make this connection but he approached it in a newly scientific manner. In May 1796, his gardener Phipps allowed him to vaccinate his eight-year-old son, James, but then once the immediate phase ended and the slight wound had healed, Jenner challenged the child's immune system with active smallpox pus in July 1796.[79] The boy did not become ill. This practice was named "vaccination" after the name Jenner invented for cowpox, *Variola vaccinae*. The role played by women in this story was passive but most important.

Jenner was received more warmly than Lady Mary and his work widely adopted, apart from a few holdouts whose spiritual descendants still bedevil the modern medical world. By 1800 vaccination was quite widespread. Freeing the public from the grip of smallpox was an enormous achievement. Two hundred years later, scientists have now eradicated the virus causing the disease, making it a defunct threat. They have retained one vial with living virus in case it is ever needed for more research. It is locked in a secret lab to protect it from medical terrorism.

Another poorly understood serious affliction was the "dropsy." William Withering (1741–1799) was also a country doctor in Staffordshire who wanted to be able to do more for his patients. He too had been very well educated for the time and was a consultant at the Birmingham Royal Infirmary. Withering belonged to the Lunar Society, a group of the most forward-thinking men in the country. He was open to ideas and particularly interested in botany. Withering wrote a flora of his county.

As people age their hearts often fail. Their bodies swell with retained fluid and cease to function properly. The condition was called "dropsy" in the eighteenth century. Withering was intrigued by the success of an old woman near his home who could somehow turn this around when he could do nothing. Overcoming the intrinsic snobbery and class prejudice of his time, he asked her what she was doing. She showed him the leaves of the foxglove plant, *Digitalis purpurea,* a wildflower found in the surrounding fields and forests.

She steeped the leaves in hot water and gave the tea to the patients. Neither she nor the educated doctor knew how the tea worked but the improvement was undeniable. Like Jenner, Withering made this information available to other doctors in 1785 and digitalis with its derivatives is still one of the most useful drugs in medicine and cardiology in the twenty first century.[152]

Speculating about whether such advances in medicine would have happened if it had all been left to women is futile. Although they sometimes got close to an answer, they were never able to reach the threshold of knowledge nor have the time to observe the progression of a disease in its entirety. No one ever developed their capacity for abstract thinking because men thought female brains were not strong enough to cope with it. To us it sounds absurd but that attitude persisted well into the nineteenth century.

Treating common ailments with herbal remedies still persisted in the countryside. For example, country people knew that the seeds of the poppy flower, *Papaver somniferum*, were analgesic and that eating poppy heads could control pain. Thomas Hardy tells us this in *Far From the Madding Crowd*.[103] Sergeant Troy is injured and finds some poppies before going to bed. It is now illegal to grow *P. somniferum* in private gardens in the United Kingdom.

Even in this endeavor, women were not completely free of competition. The monasteries offered care for the sick as part of their mission. In its day, the idea that giving a wounded man food and water could keep him alive while the wounds healed was in itself quite revolutionary. Monks discovered nursing. How and when women took over nursing is another matter. Most monastery gardens had special plots for physic where the apothecary brother grew his medicinal plants and then processed them to keep over time. This enabled him to treat the members of his community without needing women. Some really strict orders would not even allow female animals on the premises.

One of the earliest and most famous monastery "physic" gardens was at the Benedictine abbey in St. Gallen in Switzerland. It was laid out in the year 900 CE and the plans are still available. Physic, or sometimes physick, is an old term for drugs. (This is of course the basis of the term "physician.") The monks used their plants to treat the patients in their hospital, though what could be done in a hospital back then was utterly different from what is done now. They were simply places of comfort to the dying. Women religious also had physic gardens, the most notable being that of Hildegard, the abbess of Bingen.

WOMEN'S RELIGIOUS CONGREGATIONS

Speaking of abbesses, there was one domain which demonstrated that all the strictures about women's unfitness to handle complex problems were completely specious, and that was being an abbess in charge of a large convent or abbey. Making sure that the congregation did what they were supposed to do, the abbess also had to negotiate with prelates, handle and acquire property, maintain discipline, settle the frequent clashes of personality that are bound to occur in cloistered communities, see that there was enough to eat, that rents were collected and children instructed required very considerable management ability. There could be more than a hundred women in these communities. Abbesses usually came from the aristocracy, indicating that girls also learned leadership, perhaps by watching their adult relatives in action. It seems no one ever questioned such women's fitness for these impressive responsibilities.

Women of this rank ran schools, religious establishments, and other large organizations "below the radar," as it were. Their success excited little if any comment. Almost all of them were celibate and perhaps that had something to do with their capacity to do this work.

THE PRACTICE OF MEDICINE

One can see from the discussion above that the current rigid boundaries between physicians, nurses, and ancillary personnel were not like that in the early modern era. One of the very first steps in creating a little order in this situation was to establish guilds, organizations limited to persons of the same trade and having recognized credentials. New members also had to be accepted by the existing membership, making the process very subjective. The physicians had one such guild, the barber-surgeons had one too, and the apothecaries had another. They all excluded women.

MIDWIFERY

Women were the ones who produced babies and for eons the event was presided over by other women. "Male midwives" emerged from the pack of general physicians in the sixteenth century, spearheaded by Dr. Peter Chamberlen's discovery of forceps to assist the delivery of an infant whose head was stuck.[107] Other male doctors were already beginning to attend confinements but this was such a significant advance that the Chamberlens never let a pair of forceps out of their hands for five generations. The family was Huguenot and had fled to London in 1569, before the St. Bartholomew Day's Massacre.

These tools and the technique gave them a monopoly but also introduced the idea that male physicians were more fitted to supervise labor and delivery than an ignorant midwife. In order to underscore this difference, the very name of the discipline was changed to the grander sounding "obstetrics:" "one standing before." Looking back from the scientific heights of the present, they were probably about as ignorant as each other but this allowed men to plant a flag.

Intentional termination of pregnancy was a controversial topic for as long as there have been religious creeds and varying views about life. Huge forces were at work. These positions do not even take into account spontaneous fetal wastage in the earliest embryonic stages, possibly about 15% of all zygotes.

Only when a woman's life was valued for her talents and ability to perform other functions than childbearing did abortion become central to public life. Broadly speaking, this coincided with the move to the cities during the eighteenth and nineteenth centuries. A poor man working for a pittance in a factory did not need fifteen children. In fact, the fewer children he had to feed, the better. The urban population was maintained by new waves of rural people moving to the cities.

After these sweeping generalizations, it is necessary to understand that abortion always took place, often surreptitiously, for many reasons. The principal one was social opprobrium. If an unmarried woman or a woman whose husband was away for a long time became pregnant, she faced truly punitive ostracism. Village women herbalists were the ones who could help to terminate the pregnancy. In the cities, poorly educated women also took care of an unwanted pregnancy but often by direct action in the uterus.

The most commonly used drug was an extract of "pennyroyal," *Mentha pulegium*. The terminology tended to be euphemistic, such as "restoring the menses." Several of the books intended for women included recipes for doing just that.

Some of the herbal mixtures and their uses sound a bit dubious when read in the harsh light of the twenty first century. Trotula, the eleventh century Salernian midwife, who may or may not have written the treatise on *The Diseases of Women*, recommended, for instance: "A sprout of rose with juice of violets and endive" against excessive flow of the menses, among a variety of other recipes using other plants for the same problem.[65] On the other hand, scantiness of the periods may be remedied by a potion of "iris root, catnip, rue, and fennel, well cleaned and cooked in wine," or yet a mixture of "tansy, clover, and wormwood cooked in butter and placed over the navel."

If a woman was not menstruating at all, she was to bathe and take diuretics like fennel, wheathead, parsley, or rock parsley cooked in wine. If the womb had hardened and therefore the menses cannot be produced: "shredded wool soaked in a bull's gallbladder, powdered soda, juice of parsley or hyssop and pressed into the shape of a man's penis was to be inserted into the vagina." The book is very explicit. The eleventh century did not mince words.

The legal restrictions against abortion in the United States were a product of the nineteenth century. Previously, abortion in the first trimester, before "quickening," was allowed as part of an effort to control the size of the family. Apart from religious and moral concerns, the medical societies wanted to curtail the activities of untrained practitioners, including abortionists and consolidate all medical interventions into their own profession. Racism also played a role. If white American women failed to produce enough children, the nation was at risk of being overrun by "undesirable" groups. These restrictions began in the 1850s and prevailed until very recently.

WOMEN'S ROLES SHRINK

With the practice of medicine now firmly in male hands, middle- and upper-class women were becoming less and less useful. Fewer of them needed to know how to garden, to milk a cow, to cook, or care for poultry. The pressure of the times was leading them into purely ornamental roles. Centuries would pass before women would reclaim their former standing in horticulture or medicine. Echoes of that uselessness persisted down into the twentieth century. As Virginia Woolf later put it in the opening of *Mrs Dalloway*, Mrs Dalloway's contribution to an evening party at her house was to arrange the flowers.[153]

With the inexorable spread of cities, small independent farms began to be replaced by market gardens, such as those in the villages of Brompton and Kensington surrounding London. This arrangement only lasted as long as London's population was stable but when great increases occurred in the mid-nineteenth century, such villages were subsumed into Greater London and market gardening was pushed farther away, further separating the consumer from the production of food. Countrywomen worked in these gardens, usually assisting their husbands.

Plant lore receded into remote rural areas. Much of what had always been done in the home was now being done commercially by other people, relieving a city housewife of her former responsibilities. Pharmaceutical chemists compounded remedies rather than a village housewife. Apothecaries had always occupied an intermediate position between chemists and physicians, compounding equally awful remedies as everyone else.

In the United Kingdom, any possibility of growing one's own food was limited in a city by the tiny plots on which houses were built. The majority of the really poor people lived in tenements with no land at all but there was one possibility. The bits of land left over when the new railways cut though the edges of town were the property of the community in which they were found. These municipalities often permitted residents to take charge of these "allotments," whether for a nominal fee or no fee at all, so long as they improved them by growing something on them. It could be flowers or vegetables or both. There was always a good deal of competition for these scarce resources and the gardeners were very competitive.

There was no question that allotments were working-class male preserves. Women were tolerated as guests but a competent gardener could save the family money by growing useful vegetables. During the wars, women filled in for their absent men but returned to their previous subservient roles as soon as the men came back. Women taking over the allotments was an important part of the war effort and has been well described by Ursula Buchan in *A Green and Pleasant Land.*[89]

If a large middle-class house came with a garden, almost everyone employed a male gardener to maintain it. If the homeowner had a strong sense of style, he might have commissioned a male landscape architect like John Claudius Loudon to lay it out.

Much of the substance of this book is to see how women worked around these conventions to take care of their own gardens without being "unladylike." There is minor irony in the fact that during these various epochs when women were being shut out of any useful contributions, they turned to their gardens for respite and refuge in some way or another.

NINETEENTH-CENTURY ATTITUDES TOWARD WOMEN

At no point in history did it seem outlandish for European women to work hard in gardens until the highly anomalous mores of the Victorian era, with its unprecedented prudishness and social requirements, took hold. Upper-class women, working-class women and the emerging professional and middle-class women had always gardened but the weight of the shift in attitude fell most heavily on middle- and aspiring middle-class women.

Aristocratic women could more or less do what they wanted, as they were so safely established in European society. Working-class women had no choice. They either worked or they starved. It was simple. However, if your father were a duke or your husband an earl, getting your hands dirty in the soil was a charming eccentricity.

One still finds seventeenth-century upper-class women whose impressive involvement with gardens was noted in their day. Lucy Russell, Countess of Bedford, whose garden so deeply inspired Sir William Temple, as he tells us in the *Gardens of Epicurus* and Sophia of Hannover, who created the internationally famous gardens at Herrenhausen, come immediately to mind.[143] It is all the more interesting then, that the best-known authors on garden history fail to show women as playing any creative part in the gardens of the eighteenth century. A notable exception was Luise Gotheim, who in her *History of Garden Art* (1927) duly recognized various German queens' and princesses' interest in gardens and garden design.[38]

A striking example of this was the Margravine of Baden. Her husband, the Margrave, employed Joseph

Gottlieb Koelreuter, 1733–1806, as director of his botanical gardens in Karlsruhe. Koelreuter was a highly educated physician and utterly obsessed scholar of natural history. He had joined the margrave's staff after a stint in St Petersburg, curating the Tsar's collection of fish. Zoology was not his natural inclination. He preferred botany and in particular was studying the effects of cross-breeding in *Nicotiana*, the tobacco plant. Despite the huge logistical difficulties, he succeeded in transporting his precious seedlings from Russia to Germany without grievous loss.

The point of this rather long anecdote lies in the role played by the margravin, Caroline. The estate's gardeners were devout Catholics and very alarmed by what they saw their new boss doing, taking pollen from one flower and placing it on the style of another. This was sacrilege. Only God could create a new plant. They complained to the margrave, but his wife intervened and protected Koelreuter. She was very interested in science. Alas, she developed a serious illness and a day or two after she died Koelreuter was sent packing from the botanical garden. In spite of that, he was still allowed to teach at the university.

It was the women with a much more tenuous grip on society who had the most to lose and were firmly regimented both by their families and society. The books by Horwood and Way describe very effectively how women gardened across all the epochs covered here. One might be tempted to believe that the strictures considered here constituted much ado about nothing but real "hands in the earth" gardening was not considered "ladylike" for a long time. [110, 149]

To find a useful comparison with how the Victorians treated women, one could turn to earlier centuries in China. Wealthy men controlled their women by literally crippling them, binding their feet in childhood so they could only ever hobble around. The toes were tucked under the soles and kept in place by tight bonds. Eventually the bones broke and the foot was frozen in that position. Women with their feet in constant pain and unable to move anywhere quickly had very little interest in rebelling or taking any social liberties.

In the Islamic world, the perceived threat posed by women is handled by keeping them in a sort of prison, purdah or in a harem. Muslim men are unequivocally dominant and wealthier ones have always exercised their control by holding women as a sort of prisoner out of sight. Genital cutting is another arm of the same program.

Whether the feet were disabled or the person kept hidden, such systems could only prevail as long as the subjects of this treatment accepted it and in most cases actively participated in it. It seems unthinkable that a mother would intentionally subject her little girls to lifelong torture but that is what happened. This procedure confirmed her daughter's place in the highest levels of society.

In nineteenth-century Europe, the bonds were not physical but just as effective. The engineering and technical discoveries in the eighteenth century caused mass shifts of people from the countryside to the towns and cities. They flocked to work in the new factories despite the ghastly conditions they found there. Instead of even the humblest of women guiding her family and keeping it healthy with her knowledge of herbs, she was now a more or less nameless and faceless drudge in the huge machine. For centuries, wealth had resided in the hands of the landed classes, based on the poorly remunerated work of their tenants and laborers. Unless a rich landowner also owned factories this shift affected his income and wellbeing.

Social shifts accompanied economic ones. As a result of the industrial revolution, the middle classes began amassing money and status at a rate never before thought possible. Whole cities like Birmingham and Sheffield appeared as if out of nowhere, yet the very notion of a middle class was almost an oxymoron. There were landed gentry and the peasants. The small number of better-educated members of the community, such as doctors, lawyers or clergymen, were usually included as honorary members of the gentry but only on sufferance and usually kept at arms' length.

Think of Jane Austen's Reverend Mr. Collins and Lady de Bourgh in *Pride and Prejudice*.[76] The acid test was whether such persons were allowed to join the aristocrats at their dining table, to say nothing of where they might be allowed to sit once there. Servants of intermediate rank, yet still genteel like governesses, were given a tray of food to eat in their rooms. Everyone else had to go to the kitchen. One exquisite cameo of this treatment is seen in Sir Walter Scott's *Waverley*.[135] The bailiff, Baillie MacWheeble, was permitted to sit at the bottom of the laird's table but tried very hard to efface himself by pushing his chair all the way back and taking an almost horizontal dining position.

If it were difficult for the men in these new middle positions, how much more difficult it was for their wives. The gardener Joseph Paxton had a very special relationship with his employer, the Duke of Devonshire. Aristocrats did not usually dine with the working classes but the duke invited Paxton to dine with him on occasion. Mrs. Paxton was tacitly excluded. It was simply a man-to-man meal, always to discuss the grounds at Chatsworth. This was a fairly distinct situation in which a working-class man had climbed by reason of his exceptional skill and hard work into the middle class but his wife was unable to keep up with him. Paxton's wife remained the daughter of a miller but Sarah Paxton was very wise and never complained. When her husband was traveling with the duke, Sarah quietly took charge of Joseph's responsibilities, making sure bills were paid and the gardeners kept in order. Aristocratic attitudes and such social hierarchy endured for centuries and still have echoes in modern social behavior.

Poor things, newly enriched lower-class ladies were in a social bind. High-born ladies were not interested in receiving the wives of iron founders or merchants and the latter despised country women or anyone in the next ranks beneath them. It would be demeaning to associate with such women. Trade in any form was anathema to the aristocrats and this snobbery trickled down to the next level.

No wonder that they girded themselves about with etiquette etched in stone, making their daughters completely unassailable socially. Thomas Bowdler epitomized the era with his edition of Shakespeare carefully purged of any possible sexual innuendo or scatological reference. Dr. Bowdler made sure nothing that would make a maidenly cheek blush was ever allowed to see the light of day.[136] These young women were pure, they were ignorant and they were utterly useless. That was of course the point. The middle classes were consolidating their position in society by outdoing their social betters. Women were to be solely ornamental. The small amount of latitude they were afforded in the more unbuttoned previous eras was cut off.

Once again, Jane Austen skewered the contrast between the generations in a novel like *Sense and Sensibility*.[77] Worldly men used the adjective "missish" to describe the exaggeratedly shocked behavior of virginal young ladies toward perceived indelicacies.

2

EIGHTEENTH-CENTURY ENGLAND

WOMEN CREATE GARDENS OF THEIR OWN

For scholars concerned with the eighteenth century in general and with women's history in particular, studies of the development of the English garden present a strange anomaly. In contrast to both earlier and later periods when women's gardening activities are, to some extent at least, acknowledged, women are conspicuously absent from general garden histories of the eighteenth century. Why should that be?

From the writings of garden historians, gardening in the eighteenth century in England appears to have been a male preserve. Books on garden history, whether general surveys or monographs on eighteenth century gardens, are concerned with, one might almost say blinded by that splendid English creation — the "landscape garden" or park.[1] The discussion in the eighteenth century upon which garden historians rely heavily, centers around the desirability

of making the most of the natural terrain, letting the
"genius of the place," in Pope's phrase, suggest the contours
of the garden, and doing away with "unnatural" devices
such as topiary work.

These ideas were the natural swing of the pendulum
from the fashion of one century to another. Complex
designs resembling embroidery, meant to be seen from the
second story of a house, were the dominant garden style in
the seventeenth century, so it is not surprising that the
owners of fine properties wanted to get as far away from it
as they could. In my lifetime (JMT) growing up in the
London of the 1940s, anything to do with the reign of
Queen Victoria was anathema. Only just now are we
starting to appreciate the enormous contributions the
Victorians made, though we seldom reproduce their
furniture or gardens. That may need another hundred
years.

Perhaps the most famous English designer of the
eighteenth century landscape park was Lancelot Brown, also
known as "Capability," since he would walk the estate and
often ended by saying "This land has capabilities, my lord."
An appreciation of scale represents a significant difference
between male and female observers but is probably not an
absolute. This too may be connected with cultural norms.
Once women entered the fields of architecture and
landscape architecture, their ideas soared.

Women had never been expected to deal with very
large-scale construction. Even wealthy ones led very
circumscribed lives in relatively small spaces and had never
been involved with building an edifice, a canal, a railroad, or
a bridge. That was the province of men, by design.

The panoply of plants available to gardeners began to

expand very markedly as the seventeenth century gave way to the next one. Waves of new trees and shrubs were coming to Europe primarily from North America but as the century progressed, increasingly from Asia and Africa. The neat geometrical designs in the parterres had depended on native plants and low-growing shrubs like box for contrasting color. Noblemen's gardeners sometimes even used painted gravel for extra effect.

Another facet of these changes was the idea that a prudent man planted trees for his heirs rather than merely to please himself during his own lifetime. With increasing security, it was possible to consider that the family would survive into future generations. Posterity became much more important.

Increasingly, the eighteenth-century ideal incorporated the surrounding landscape into the vistas of the garden and eventually transformed the garden itself into a landscaped park by creating lakes and hills where none existed before. In the literature, names of great garden and landscape designers, like Henry Wise, Charles Bridgeman, William Kent, John Vanbrugh, and Humphrey Repton are bracketed with those of great landowners who left a powerful mark on their own landscapes working with professionals: Lord Burlington and Alexander Pope at Chiswick, the Earl of Carlisle at Castle Howard, the Duke of Marlborough at Blenheim, Henry Hoare at Stourhead, Richard Cobham at Stowe, and the Dormers, father and son, at Rousham. All these parks are still places of pilgrimage, even in the twenty-first century.

English gentlemen of the eighteenth century returned from their fashionable "grand tours" of the European continent with treasures of classical statuary. These treasures, together with copies and adaptations of Greco-Roman temples and other classical motifs, were erected on carefully chosen, often symbolic sites in the ever larger and more consciously landscaped parks surrounding ever-smaller country houses.[2]

Many of the parks resulting from this eighteenth century English contribution to art and to the aesthetic pleasures of life have endured for two hundred years, even though the actual dwellings are now put to other uses, like the public school at Stowe. The descendants of their creators, pleasure-seeking visitors as well as garden historians, wander through these parks in England and through adaptations of them in other parts of the world. The longevity of eighteenth-century landscape parks is indeed remarkable in contrast to the relatively ephemeral characteristics of gardens of other centuries.

Where then, were the women? It would seem from the dearth of references to English women in the literature on the history of the eighteenth century garden that they were simply not involved in its creation, although they are known to have understood and enjoyed its advantages. Paintings depict ladies appreciating the elegant walks and secluded shrubberies.

One letter stated that "On a tour of the garden at St. Paul's Waldon Bury in Oxfordshire, where the Countess of --- pointed out to us the concern she had formerly taken in the shrubs, and flower beds, the lawns, the alcoves and the walks, even the assistance her own hand had lent to individual articles."[5]

The significant clue to the puzzle of women's absence from the literature of eighteenth-century garden history may lie in the Countess of Strathmore's interest in certain very specific aspects of the garden. It is the flowers, shrubs, and walks that predominantly interested her. The famous park like innovations were the hallmark of the eighteenth century but the judiciously planted trees; small woods, lakes, and streams and architectural structures like bridges, temples, statuary, and grottoes, all passed her by. To put it bluntly, she had done her duty in providing heirs for posterity and could be pardoned for wanting to enjoy the garden here and now.

In fact, although the Countess of Strathmore is the only woman mentioned in the general literature on eighteenth-century garden history, she is not unique. Upper-class women gardened like the Countess, both as supervisors and with their own hands.

The fragmentary accounts of eighteenth-century ladies' gardening contrasts with the elaborate historical and literary treatment of landscape design that has been the preoccupation of scholars. Women continued to work on the flower garden throughout this century but this activity escaped historical and literary attention as being too mundane.

Here are a few examples of their work.

At the beginning of the century, in 1707, John Lawrence (under the name of Charles Evelyn) wrote *The Lady's Recreation* in order to encourage women to lay out orange trees, grass plots, and statues, yet he did not find it necessary to give directions for growing the commonest flowers, such as foxgloves, garden mallows, scabious, fennel, double lady's smock, and others. These, he said: "Every Country Dame has in her garden and knows how to sow, plant and propagate."[13] In the middle of the century, a writer in *The Ladies Magazine* took it for granted that ladies would be growing flowers and gave advice on how to have tulips and lilies blooming by Christmas.

Lady Mary Coke wrote in her diary about her garden in Notting Hill in December 1767: "The weather continues fine and pleasant. I planted many flowers and some plants but saw Nobody the whole day."[19] and again, "On Thursday, when I came home, they told me one of the cows had broke into the new walk and had eat up almost all the shrubs; 'tis vexatious, but these things are trifles."[20] The very next morning she was out "planting a great many flowers."[21] Lady Mary put in honeysuckle to "gratify her sister's nose,"[22] cut her finger pruning her jessamines and tells her sister in November, 1768: "I have still several flowers undecayed — but much as I love them, at this season they seem so cold and uncomfortable."[23, 24]

In 1786, Hannah More wrote "I work in my garden 2 or 3 hours every day...I am rather proud of my pinks and Roses..." and "Charming weather for transplanting Roses: I can't help envying people who are at their own gardens. Now is the time to take your pot herbs out of your pleasure ground, and your Pinks from your kitchen garden. Both will behave better in their proper stations."[25, 26] Hannah More was a friend of Hester Thrale's in Streatham, and part of that very stimulating group around Samuel Johnson. He was fond of her though his favorite in that hospitable household was Fanny Burney.

The "Ladies of Llangollen," Lady Eleanor Butler and Lady Sarah Ponsonby, daughters of prominent Irish aristocratic families, planted "a great quantity of Primroses on the bank by the shed" and they sowed their pinks seeds before walking round the shrubbery where they "beheld the loveliest moon in the softest richest clouds."[27, 28] The younger of the two, Sarah Ponsonby, specialized in geraniums and owned eighty varieties.[29]

In Grasmere, Dorothy Wordsworth "sowed the flowers." Her brother William, she wrote laconically in her diary, "helped me" and later she "brought home lemon thyme and several other plants and planted them by moonlight."[30, 31]

Harriet Stratfield left a notebook from the year 1773, in which she described her many planting and gardening plans.[32]

About one hundred and eighty women subscribed in their own name to Furber's famous flower catalogues. They were able to order flower seeds from his Kensington Nursery in 1730.[33]

Clearly, eighteenth century ladies gardened. Throughout the century, flower gardens flourished under female hands, while the celebrated innovation of the landscape park flourished under male direction. Women's letters and diaries describing their flower-growing thus tells us a little more of what gardens were actually like. They also corroborate evidence from paintings. For example, the wonderful Thomas Robins paintings of flower gardens of the 1750s or the garden of the Drake-Brockman family in Kent, ca. 1745, which shows a flower border surrounding a typical classical rotunda in a landscaped park with an artificial lake are typical of the period.[34]

Women's gardening also corroborates the thrust of the exhibition on The Garden: A Celebration of 1,000 Years of British Gardening (Summer 1979) at the Victoria and Albert

Museum in London, which, while ignoring women's contribution, emphasized the fact that the flower garden had not disappeared in the eighteenth century.[35] Eighteenth-century ladies were concerned primarily with flowers but they were not unaware of the new landscape ideas. Hester Thrale, in 1777, for example, was sharply critical of the new fad for "improvements," and condemned Pope's inconsistencies. She wrote: "Pope says Lord Bathurst's gardens should have some Mounts, because the place lies flat. In the name of wonder what would he have seen from the mounts? I don't like Pope's taste in gardening. 'Consult the Genius of the Place in All' was a rule he did not observe," and she quoted with relish Dr. Johnson's quip on grottoes: "Do you not think the grotto a delightful habitation Dr. Johnson?" "Yes Madam, for a Toad."[36, 37]

Other women incorporated landscape ideals when they were in a position so to do. Queen Caroline, as we know, had been an early employer of Charles Bridgeman. She had requested him to refashion Kensington Gardens and Hyde Park, planning avenues and the Serpentine and thus bringing him and the new landscape designs fame.[38] Humbler ladies, somewhat lower down the social scale, who recorded their thoughts on gardening and incorporated new landscape ideals included Elizabeth Montagu, Hannah More, Lady Mary Coke, and the Ladies of Llangollen. If wealthy, and the owners of large estates, they might employ renowned landscape designers. Elizabeth Montagu employed Lancelot "Capability" Brown. On June 19, 1784 Mrs. Montagu wrote from Sandleford that "Brown's deputy has made improvements in the grounds without departing from the rural and pastoral character."[39]

In November 1767 the unmarried Lady Mary Coke sent

for the gardener of her neighbor. Lord Holland, and "gave him half a guinea for cutting some trees that opened a view into his grounds, which I had (his) permission for before he went Abroad. Since then I planted trees in my fields."[40] She also thinned trees and opened views to Chelsea, and in April 1768 she "had done a good deal of work, and have opened a view to the Town of Acton that pleases me very much."[41]

The Ladies of Llangollen's garden was internationally famous. Local tradesmen as well as foreign aristocratic landscape amateurs, such as Prince Puckler Muskau, recognized and appreciated its unique qualities. The stone artifacts among their lilacs, white broom, and moss roses included a temple where they sat to escape the midges and a font inscribed with verses they had composed.

The concept of work is the common denominator unifying their varying descriptions of the garden as a haven of delight and one that each one of these women gardeners reiterates. Planning and creating a work of art was intellectually exciting and invigorating. It was a way of dealing in reality with the botanical lore and the drawing of flowers and landscapes that had become a staple of upper-class eighteenth century girls' education.[42] The creation of the reality, often so much more difficult than the ideal described in botanical treatises or books of flower paintings, required knowledge of wind and weather, the chemistry of the soil and of the growth rate of trees and shrubs which would affect the smaller plants growing in their shade. It required a vision of the future. It required still another dimension: that is, hard physical labor.

Some of the physical labor was a little too heavy. Lady

Mary Coke obviously understood the mechanics of large-scale landscape operations better than her laborers. On one occasion she wrote: "My workmen had a very narrow escape. They were digging gravel and was just got out of the pit, when the ground above gave way. I was quite happy that No accident had happened though I had foreseen it by their method of digging and had desired them to leave it some time before they did."[43]

Motivated by an inner vision and a desire for personal achievement, many women preferred working in their gardens themselves. Caring for small plants like flowers and shrubs satisfied the need for individual creation without relying upon inefficient assistance from lazy or insensitive gardeners. For such reasons, the Ladies sacked their gardener, Richard, at Llangollen, and then did the planting themselves. Lady Eleanor wrote that they liked their garden "infinitely better empty than occupied by the drunken, idle Richard."[44] For similar reasons Lady Mary Wortley Montagu placed herself at the head of her weeder women, working from six to nine every morning.[45]

To maintain, then, that all eighteenth-century gardeners were solely preoccupied with landscape design appears to be as inaccurate as the myth that eighteenth century gardening was a male preserve. What has to be accepted is the ratio and scale of male to female involvement with its preponderance of male actors.

Both myths developed because garden historians, art historians, and literary historians have focused on change rather than on continuity. They have been preoccupied with the creation and growth of the landscape park to the point where they have lost sight of the ephemeral flower garden which had continued since the middle ages. Because of this preoccupation they have concentrated their efforts on male creativity, that is, public, large-scale, expensive, and enduring.

In Susan Bell's opinion there are three significant reasons the creation of landscape parks was indeed of far greater interest to men than to women. First: it was men who had large fortunes and possessed properties that lent themselves to extensive "improvements" with long vistas incorporating woods, lakes, and fields. Elizabeth Carter made the point by referring to her "poor little garden" and the fact that she alone as an "ancient maiden gentlewoman" could hardly keep order in it.[46] The "wilderness" so dear to the designers of the romantic landscape park had no place in little gardens kept by orderly gentlewomen of modest means. When women had the economic backing, landowners like Elizabeth Montagu or Lady Mary Coke (she who borrowed her neighbor's gardener) also landscaped their gardens into parks.

Secondly, Bell suggests that it was the young gentlemen who had the freedom to make the "grand tour" with a male companion or tutor. Returning to England filled with classical ideals, they were determined enough and wealthy enough to re-create these ideals in their properties, which they adorned with sculptures and other trophies from their journeys. Young ladies, on the whole, had neither the freedom to make a "grand tour" nor the wealth to acquire large objets d'art to scatter over property they did not own.

As Henrietta Pye said when describing the famous gardens of Twickenham for her women readers in 1775: "I have observed that ladies in general visit these places, as our young gentlemen do foreign parts... These little excursions are commonly the only travels permitted to our sex and the only way we have of becoming at all acquainted with the progress of arts...."[47] Jane Austen was writing just at the dawn of the nineteenth century but echoes these sentiments. Think of the party got up to visit Mr. Darcy's estate at Pemberly in *Pride and Prejudice.*[76]

Third, and most profound, was the power of patriarchy and primogeniture. Alexander Pope expressed this convincingly in a compelling verse. He wrote:

"Happy the man whose wish and care
  A few paternal acres bound
  Content to breathe his native air
  On his own ground"[48]

Pope, of course, was not raising questions on women's attitudes either to gardening, or indeed to life. What this particular verse provides is a key to understanding the puzzle of women's absence from the enthusiasm for the landscape park. It was indeed, the man who, not only at the time but for generations to follow, would breathe the air on the paternal acres, on his own ground. The landscaped park was planted, not for the generation which did so but for future generations. Trees and landscapes mature very slowly. The upper-class male landowner planned and planted for his male heirs.

The woman of the family knew from girlhood onwards that her future and the future of her daughters was destined to be on some other man's ground. She would not breathe her native air on her own ground nor would her garden or her daughters' gardens be bounded by maternal acres.

As Margaret Cavendish, Duchess of Newcastle had written in a splendid mixed garden metaphor in the late seventeenth century: "Daughters are but branches which by marriage are broken off from the root from whence they sprang and engrafted into the stock of another family, so that daughters are to be accounted but as moveable goods or furniture that wear out."[49] What incentive then, to plant for posterity?

The historical evidence indicates that landscape parks were the products of men who designed for posterity and who used their estates to show off and enhance their political prestige. In general, women created flower gardens that were designed only for the lifetime of the planter, providing transient artistic pleasure. Do these differences not underscore the differences in the life experience and expectations of men and women? Did the activity of men in the public sphere sharpen their desire for immortality, while the golden cage of domesticity forced ladies to garden above all as a vicarious activity?

Such a view is lent credence by the activities of Queen Caroline, a political sophisticate, who as Judith Colton has shown, was creating a political garden metaphor concerned with legitimizing the Hanoverian succession in a male political world.[50]

This perception is also perhaps endorsed by the case of Lady Mary Coke, a politician manqué of whom it was said that she "heated her brains with history as other women have done with Romance" and who worked physically in her garden in the cold of winter and till late in the evenings.[51] In the intervals, she read Catherine Macaulay's

History of England and the Parliamentary Debates of her day.

Lady Mary Wortley Montagu also took to creating a garden, when her eyesight and age curbed her former quite spectacular intellectual and literary activities. Mary Wortley Montagu wrote: "I am really as fond of my garden, as a young Author of his first play when it has been well receiv'd by the Town, and can no more forbear teazing my Acquaintance for their approbation.... Gardening is certainly the next amusement to Reading and as my sight will now permit me little of that, I am glad to form a taste that can give me so much employment and be the plaything of my Age, now my pen and needle are almost useless to me."[52] Had there had been proper refraction in those days we would not have had this tantalizing story of Lady Mary's garden. Most of her complaints were due to presbyopia, the stiffening of the natural ocular lens after the age of forty. Reading glasses would have enabled her to see perfectly clearly again.

The problem then, of women's absence from the literature of eighteenth-century garden history lies in the myth that the landscape park had ousted the flower garden. This myth is partly forged by the fact that eighteenth century landscape parks have physically endured, still to be admired two hundred years after their creation. It is reinforced by historical attention paid to this "new form" of garden in contemporary eighteenth century literature. The problem also grows out of the reality that women as a group were poor, lacked authority, and did not inherit land. As a result, they concerned themselves almost entirely with the unpolitical, unfashionable, inexpensive, private, and ephemeral flower garden.

Unlike landscapes of woods, lawns and lakes and unlike deftly sited bridges, temples and sculptures, flowers fade and disappear. The flower gardens of eighteenth-century ladies live only in their letters, in their garden notebooks, in their botanical paintings, and in their embroideries. When Herrick wrote addressing tulips he might as well have been addressing women gardeners of the eighteenth century:

"Your sisterhoods may stay.
    And smile here for your hour
    But ye must die away
    E'en as the meanest flower.
    Come virgins then, and see
    Your frailties and bemoan ye;
    For lost like these, 'twill be
    As time had never known ye.[53]

3

OPPORTUNITIES

THE GARDEN AS REFRESHMENT AND ESCAPE

Susan Bell felt very strongly that gardens were havens for women, offering quiet and peace. The garden is the intermediate space between the usually safe interior of the home and the outer world with all its unknown threats. It could be viewed as an extension of the house. Several activities could equally take place in the house or the garden, such as eating, drinking, entertaining or teaching. It is an enclosed space and enclosure is the bedrock principle in defining a garden. Almost everything one associates with gardens can be omitted in a definition but not enclosure. Even the fluid prairie style of gardens created by Jens Jensen in the early 1900s were still enclosed.

The enclosing structure could itself be a living plant, not just wood or stone. Hedges were used to separate gardens in town and countryside alike. For fifty years, imperial India was cut off from the minor principalities by a twenty-foot deep thorny hedge running a thousand miles down the center of the country. It was pierced at intervals by customs posts but was otherwise completely impenetrable. The purpose was to catch poor natives who bought salt more cheaply outside the imperial districts where it was heavily taxed.

With enclosure in mind, recent scholars have examined the functions of gates, doors, and windows in women's history with gardens. All these objects work two ways, to go in or to come out and thus frame attitudes and the approach to a landscape. A garden can then appear to be a transitional space, with all that implies. Being in a garden could encourage a nervous woman to go outside into the street by herself. The famous Victorian traveler Gertrude Bell used that metaphor in her book about Syria, leaving the safety of the garden to go to the Middle East.[80]

These attitudes have been teased out by examining the correspondence and literature of women who recorded what they felt at different times. The emotions evoked by gardens range very widely from safety and security to joy and delight. Physical exhilaration and the creation of beauty came to mean a lot to women who were cooped up most of the time. If weeds get the upper hand, add frustration to this list.

The positive emotions are so powerful they can lead to improved healing after medical treatment. These responses seem to be mediated largely by vision. It is not necessary to be out in the open air to benefit from them, though that is of course a powerful enhancer, particularly if you factor in fragrance and birdsong.

Psychologists have published reliable studies showing that a patient in a hospital who can see a garden or even simply a tree from their room stays a shorter time after treatment than one who only looks out on a brick wall.[127] The work is so compelling that new hospitals are being built with such views as a matter of course. Two new hospitals built recently in San Francisco offer a view of a small terrace garden or some plants from every room, even the Intensive Care Unit. The author of the original studies, Dr. Clair Marcus, was a consultant to the building committees.

O. Henry wrote a poignant short story based on this fact without even knowing its scientific basis.[106] He tells of a young girl seriously ill with pneumonia in Chicago in the early twentieth century. Until the 1930s, there was no effective treatment for pneumonia. It was early in the winter. The patient said she would die when the last leaf fell from the tree outside her window. Her distraught neighbor, an elderly artist, stayed up one night and painted a realistic leaf on the wall behind the tree in hopes of keeping her alive. This heartened her so much she recovered. The poor man then got pneumonia and died himself.

Many women wrote their books and letters in little garden structures, such as a gazebo or a "shed." Dorothy Wordsworth built one on the small rise in their cottage garden in Grasmere soon after she and her brother William moved in.[30] Words and ideas seemed to flow better in the relative silence of a garden, though it is well known that Jane Austen wrote her novels while in the midst of the family hubbub.

Children could play alone safely in the garden as long as they did not stray outside where they could be kidnapped by gypsies. The values of order, neatness and respect for nature could be imparted to children using the garden as a classroom. Being given a tiny plot of their own to cultivate was one way of getting them excited and yet teach them the virtues of patience. They had to learn not to pull up their radishes until the root was ready. The formal study of botany was another way to bring some discipline into their development.

Gardens are still ideal places for teaching. The department of mathematics at the University of California at Berkeley developed a practical syllabus of teaching young children elementary mathematical principles by working them out in order to grow flowers and vegetables in a garden.[126] Even the simplest plot requires the gardener to be able to count and measure. Learning to do this in a garden makes it fun and painless.

BOTANY BECOMES A SUITABLE SCIENCE FOR WOMEN

Just as men had slowly muscled in on women's healing prerogatives, so did the study of botany become the wedge which led women back into the practice of horticulture. It was genteel and non-threatening. Botany, Greek for pasture grasses, was first taught as a separate subject from general "natural history" at the University of Oxford in the mid-seventeenth century, before anywhere else. The Scottish botanist Robert Morison was appointed the first professor in 1669 and laid out the handsome botanical garden, still a focal point at the lower end of High Street opposite Magdalen College, along the River Cherwell.

This was by no means the beginning of botany as we know it but marked an important milestone. For more than three hundred years, until 1899 when aspirin was first synthesized, the teaching of therapeutics was largely the teaching of botany. Plants were the main source of drugs. Colleges which maintained excellent botanical gardens taught excellent medicine. The students were all male as were the teachers. The knowledge of plants had become systematized and made into a proto-scientific discipline. Women were no longer welcome except to protect the plants by weeding.

One mainstay of teaching was the herbarium, a collection of pressed and dried plants affixed to very strong paper and carefully labelled with everything that was known about each one. It allowed the scholar to see every organ of the plant very clearly. This collection was critically important, establishing a "gold standard" for resolving future controversies and disagreements. The herbarium was also useful for teaching in the seasons when plants no longer bloomed and it was too wet or cold to go outside for lectures.

Properly cared for, these papers and the desiccated remnants can survive for a very long time. The University of Oxford Department of Plant Sciences has at least one specimen found on the coast of Western Australia by the "pirate of exquisite mind," Captain William Dampier, in 1699. Weak echoes of preparing an herbarium descended through the echelons of female botanical dilettantes with their pretty albums. Properly constructed herbaria are still necessary and remain essential for professional botanists and taxonomists.

A very remarkable derivative of the herbarium is the set of completely realistic glass models of flowers created between 1887 and 1936 by two Czech watchmakers, Leopold and Rudolf Blaschka, father and son. The flowers are permanently on exhibit at Harvard's Peabody Museum.

The university commissioned them for teaching when the actual flowers were out of bloom. There are 4300 models in all. Two hundred years before that Mary Delany had done something similar with paper. (See page 86)

BOTANICAL CLASSIFICATION

Until Carolus Linnaeus published *Species Plantarum* in 1753, scholars were having increasing difficulty in discussing plants because of uncertainty about their names.[124] More and more plants were being discovered whether at home or abroad. One of the few things everyone agreed upon was that the official names should be in Latin, the lingua franca of the academic world. New plants were discovered which looked a bit like some previously seen but were not exactly the same. Both the vernacular and Latin names were modified to represent the differences and that led to long polysyllabic descriptions of increasing complexity which helped no one.

Linnaeus' system was the equivalent of Alexander the Great cutting the Gordian knot. It was not the only system and in fact was not even a "natural" system but had the advantage of being easily understood and used in practice. Each organism, whether plant or animal, was known by a binomial label, the first one being the genus and the second one the species. Fitting a plant with one of these names depended on counting the flower's sexual organs. *Mentha pulegium*, pennyroyal, is an example of the binomial system.

The genus is *Mentha*, or mint, the species is *pulegium*, or pennyroyal. Human beings are labelled *Homo sapiens*, a much disagreed-upon designation. Human history shows that wisdom has been in short supply most of the time.

When it came to teaching women about science in the nineteenth century, botany was readymade for the task. Their supposedly fragile brains would not be strained by studying flowers and they would not be exposed to coarse animal realities like reproduction. It was pretty and it was safe. For some reason, all the Mrs. Grundys turned a blind eye to the fact that Linnaeus built his system on sexual differences, counting the number of stamens or male organs, versus the number of styles, female organs, in his classification. ("Mrs Grundy" was a character from a play by Thomas Morton in 1798, *Speed The Plough*, who was exaggeratedly conventional. The name became a figure of speech.) The biggest danger lay in the person of the teacher if he were a handsome young man and the least bit unscrupulous.

Perhaps one of the most fortuitous uses of botany and the sexuality of plants was when the Abbé Gregor Mendel, 1822–1884, began his study of transmitted characteristics. At first he kept a series of black and white mice, crossing them and counting the offspring by color. The bishop came to the abbey of the Thomaskirche in Brno on a surprise visit and was shocked to see what Mendel was doing. He forbade it at once. Mendel very cleverly turned to breeding vegetable peas: green and yellow, tall and short, ones with grey flowers and ones with white, muttering as he did, "Plants have sex too." Mendel had grown up on a farm.

VICTORIAN PRUDERY

This is not the place in which to inveigh against the monumental disconnect between the reality of life and the perception of what certain women should see and learn but it influenced what women could and could not do in gardens for a long time. Girls growing up on farms would have had some inkling of natural processes but girls in towns did not have a clue, in spite of the fact that almost all children were born at home until the early twentieth century. Hospitals were still incredibly dangerous places at the time, as noted in the comments on Semelweiss. What did anyone imagine was going on when mother disappeared upstairs and a new baby somehow appeared as if by magic? Many mixed messages were being sent at the same time. The prime one was that if one did not talk about it, then nothing had happened.

The new emphasis on maidenly ignorance and purity reflected the fact that in one way or another, women were still chattels. The degree to which that was enforced varied over the centuries. In systems in which women were chattels, sexual purity was the primary incentive. Men were thought to be at the mercy of all women's constant sexual snares, voluntary or otherwise and powerless to withstand them. All evil came from Eve. (There is no etymological connection between Eve and evil.) It was essential to minimize that in every possible way. The most important reason for insisting on this was that a man could not know if the children in his marriage were actually his. Judaism enshrines this reality in recognizing who is a Jew. One is only a Jew if one's mother were Jewish. No one can be sure about the father.

In Islam, the innate and uncontrollable seductiveness of women, even if unintentional, remains a central tenet to this day. They have to cover their hair at the very least, if not the rest of their form with shapeless clothes to hide its outline. Women's hair is a highly charged secondary sexual characteristic. People eventually moved past that overt discrimination in Western society, but only to a certain point. Rules about women's exteriors may have softened, but her behavior was still subject to the same iron laws. They were still chattels.

Keeping young girls ignorant and free of sexual knowledge became a mark of gentility and measured the distance the family had come from the farm. These girls occupied themselves with harmless ladylike pursuits, one of which was botany. The neutral language of "stamens" and "styles" obscured the fact that those were sexual organs. There was even a health benefit to this pastime. Collecting flowers meant going out in the open air for walks.

Once again, one must remember that these restrictions applied to middle- and upper-middle-class women or in any class where property was involved. In an attempt to be more genteel than these elegant ladies, great armies of imitators followed in their footsteps, condemning girls and women to stultifying seclusion and meaningless, frivolous occupations. Take Jane Austen's *Emma*, with the illegitimate Miss Harriet as a perfect example of such a young lady.[75] Harriet's foolishness led to her rejecting a splendid young farmer who genuinely loved her for a fantasy about the local very ambitious clergyman, a fantasy promoted by the upper-class Emma herself.

Social customs had been a bit looser and more robust in previous decades. Young women were encouraged to attend the lectures and demonstrations of savants and expected to know something about new sciences like chemistry as they unfolded in the latter part of the eighteenth century. They could read the great writers who pulled no punches in describing life. The men around them were often licentious, leaving little to the imagination.

Forty years later, in *The Tenant of Wildfell Hall* (1848), Ann Bronte demonstrated this behavior and its effect on women.[87] Behavior changed when prudery took over, epitomized by Mr. Bowdler and his editions of Shakespeare in the early nineteenth century without sexual innuendos or curse words.[136] Even men had to mind their "p"s and "q"s, at least in public. Women's fashion changed to mirror the new rules. The very revealing necklines of the late eighteenth and early nineteenth century dresses gave way to high necks and long sleeves, except for glamorous occasions like balls. This style did have one advantage. It was much warmer than its predecessors.

Throughout it all, botany was a way of enlivening the daily round. Finding a plant, pressing it between sheets of paper to dry it for later study and very often drawing or painting the flowers and seeds were all fully acceptable tasks. Using the many highly simplified and sugarcoated guidebooks, often in verse, allowed them to identify what they had found. The young Queen Victoria's album with its watercolor paintings is still extant at Windsor. She was quite gifted. Painting flowers with accurate botanical detail and exactitude later became a lifeline for those unfortunate women of a certain class to support themselves but for whom working as a servant or in a shop was not acceptable.

Almost the only other choice they had was to be a governess. By working in flower painting they were able to be independent, something that the dreary prospect of being a governess did not offer. The idea that a gentlewoman could start a business of her own was not even on the horizon.

The closest early Victorians got to that possibility was in Mrs. Gaskell's *Cranford*.[101] The unfortunate Miss Mattie lost all her money and faced destitution. In desperation, she seized on the idea of selling tea from her house. Tea was very genteel and hardly counted as being "in trade." Her survival depended entirely on the goodwill of her friends and neighbors, not a very robust foundation.

In 1787, William Curtis founded his *Botanical Magazine*, showcasing new exotic plants as they appeared. A prime feature of the publication was the handsome colored pictures that illustrated it. Curtis was followed by dozens of other similar publications over the next fifty years, almost all of which had exceptional illustrations. Most of the pictures were painted by women artists but their names were not credited. Trying to learn who they were is very frustrating for modern scholars.

This anonymity was not confined to English and European women artists. European plant explorers based in India, like Nathaniel Wallich, employed native Indian artists to paint their collections but never recorded their names. The attitude of contempt was the same.

Once the initial picture was painted, the next step was to make an etching in black and white for the printer. When the book was being prepared for binding, each black and white print had to be colored by hand, an essential part of the process. The colourist had, on the one hand, mind-numbing, assembly-line repetition but on the other, the need for extremely careful attention to detail. Publishers had no need to pay well. For every woman who objected to the pay, five more were standing in line behind her. Working women were always seen as interlopers, greedily snatching bread out of the mouths of men with dependents yet time and again they showed their mettle in periods of crisis.

The encouragement of pure botany was the start of an

opportunity for leisured women. It became part of their repertoire of accomplishments and so devoutly to be desired. This was reflected in the extensive literature that grew up around it. Ladies wrote books about botany and gardening for other ladies. The great horticulturist John Claudius Loudon's wife Jane Webb Loudon (1807–1858) wrote a book about gardening for women while he was still alive and then wrote several more after his death to support herself.

She was the best known of the early Victorian female writers on gardening for women. Jane Loudon published her well-known book *Gardening for Ladies* in 1840. She wrote specifically for women who were concerned with small suburban villa gardens, in contrast to the Capability Brown-type of landscaped park.

John Claudius Loudon had been fascinated by Jane Webb's first book, *The Mummy!* (1827), written while she was still single and sought her out through mutual friends.[125] *The Mummy!* was science fiction depicting a utopian England of the 22nd century. She foresaw a system not unlike the Internet for communication. For all his hardheadedness, Loudon had a weakness for the fantastic and her book spoke to him immediately. Soon after their mutual friends introduced them, they got married. John only had one arm and Jane was penniless but they rose to be the premier horticultural stars of their day.

Jane Loudon admitted that she had been totally ignorant of the intricacies of horticulture before her marriage and that she owed her knowledge to the patient instruction of her husband during the first nine years of their marriage. Loudon was a sick man, in addition to having lost an arm. He had to dictate most of his prodigious books. Jane had grown up in a wealthy family but her father lost all their money and she was left to fend for herself.

Writing *The Mummy!* brought her a little security. She was a devoted wife and dedicated her book to her husband, putting the stamp of approval of middle-class respectability on the physical effort and grubbiness that might have gone against the grain of status-conscious middle-class husbands and wives. She described in detail the type of spade to be used for digging, the efficiency of a wheel barrow, and the type of manure (whether horse or steer) to be used for different soils and for different plantings. She insisted that "ladies" should wear gloves for gardening at all times.[59]

Her *Gardening for Ladies* went into many editions in England and was also issued in the United States. Out of her twenty-four published books, nine were specifically addressed to women, with titles like: *The Ladies' Companion to the Flower Garden* (1841); *Botany for Ladies* (1842); *The Lady's Country Companion or How to Enjoy a Country Life Rationally* (1845).

Quite apart from the important content of such books, one has to remember they were written entirely by hand with quill pens in cold drafty rooms, with only candles or oil lamps for light. Such diligence is truly admirable.

Fascinating as Jane Loudon's efforts to introduce the "lady" to gardening were, Susan Bell found the work of her contemporary Louisa Johnson even more interesting. Louisa Johnson's book *Every Lady Her Own Flower Gardener* was first published in 1840 and went into fourteen English editions by 1852.[60] It was then revised and adapted "for the use of American Ladies" and published in New York. It was still reprinted there as late as 1863, having already been pirated by an American publisher in 1842. The appeal of Louisa Johnson's small book was manifold.

First it was addressed specifically to "the industrious and economical only." Miss Johnson explained in her preface that she was writing at the request of women companions who could not afford a gardener but who wanted to garden themselves. One thinks of the ladies in *Cranford*. Secondly, the book was small and compact, both in physical size and in its useful technical information. It would fit comfortably into a lady's reticule while she was visiting friends or shopping for seeds. Some editions were beautifully illustrated with hand-painted flowers. Third and most significant, is Johnson's introductory philosophy on the value of gardening as a comfort for "the single of my sex," whom it "lures from dwelling too deeply upon the unavoidable disappointments and trials of life which sooner or later disturb and disquiet the heart."

Her preface tells us a great deal about the middle-class women for whom the book was composed in 1840. Johnson wrote: "I have been induced to compile this little work from hearing many of my companions regret that no single book contained a sufficiently condensed and general account of the business of a Flower Garden. 'We require,' they said,

'a work in a small compass, which will enable us to become our own gardeners. We wish to know how to go about everything ourselves, without expense, without being deluged with Latin words and technical terms and without being obliged to pick our way through multiplied publications, redolent of descriptions and not always particularly lucid. We require a practical work, telling us of useful flowers, simple modes of rearing them, simply expressed and free from lists of plants and roots which require expensive methods of preservation. Some of us have gardens, but we cannot afford a gardener. We like flowers, but we cannot attempt to take more than common pains to raise them. We require to know the hardiest flowers and to comprehend the general business of the garden, undisturbed by fear of failure and at the most economical scale of expense. Who will write us such a book?'

"I have endeavoured to meet their views." Johnson wrote, "and my plan of Floriculture may be carried into effect by any lady who can command the services of an old man, a woman, or a stout boy....The work is the result of my own experience (except a chapter on Window Gardening and Domestic Greenhouses for exotics) and I dedicate it to all of my own sex who delight in flowers and yet cannot allow themselves to enter into great expense in their cultivation."

We know little of Louisa Johnson so far except that she was a cousin of George W. Johnson, the well-known writer on horticulture but we do know a great deal about the "redundant" or "surplus" women of nineteenth century middle class England. It is indeed moving that one of them should have discussed in print so practical a remedy as gardening for the emotional turmoil and lifelong shadow that accompanied failure in the marriage market.

Louisa Johnson even pointed out the nurturing aspects of gardening, which would to some extent satisfy the repressed mothering instinct of some single women. She wrote: "A flower garden...acts upon the heart and affections as a nursery acts upon matronly feelings."

Similar advice was not offered in the aftermath of World War I, with the loss of so many millions of men. When the "Spanish flu" passed through communities at the end of the war men and women died in equal numbers but the possibility of finding a husband because of the war dropped disastrously. By then single women had already been in the workforce and equipped with skills not available to them in the mid-nineteenth century.

Almost more than any other new introductions, the bicycle and typewriter had transformed the lives of women who needed to earn their own living. Thousands ended up as typists, secretaries and schoolteachers. Secretarial work had always been the province of men. That seems quaint to us nowadays. Women with some higher education became teachers. The excellent teachers at girls' schools in London in the 1940s were unmarried because they had lost their boyfriends and fiancés in the previous war.

Following Jane Loudon and Louisa Johnson, other 19th century English women authors whose works on gardening were frequently reprinted include Theresa Earle, Alicia Amherst Cecil, Eleanour Sinclair Rohde, Ellen Willmott, and most famous of all, Gertrude Jekyll, of whom more later.

In the United States, the best-known authors in this field are Anna Warner, who wrote *Gardening by Myself* in 1872, Louisa Yeomans King, and Helena Rutherfurd Ely, whose works were well known in the first quarter of the twentieth century. A bit later came Louise Beebe Wilder and Helen Morgenthau Fox. Mrs. Wilder was a garden designer as well as a down-to-earth garden person. Mrs. Fox was almost her contemporary, but outlived her by many years. She was an expert on the lily and bred many shorter, more practical varieties but also wrote extensively on all aspects of gardening. The handsome six-foot lilies of the time were far too large for the ever-diminishing private garden. Mrs. Fox was also an authority on culinary herbs, growing as many as she could find and employing a French chef full-time at her estate in Bedford, New York to cook with them as widely as possible.

It was by no means only Victorian spinsters who took up gardening as a satisfying interest. Letters, diaries, and memoirs of British upper- and middle-class women, whether single or married, who did not make a career as authors on the subject of gardening, refer to their work in the garden as a pleasurable and satisfying occupation.

Jane Austen's women were no gardeners. The closest she came to having a woman gardener was Miss Eliot, whose "special flowers" were discussed with the male gardener in *Persuasion* and the poor relation, Fanny Price, who was dispatched to cut the dead blooms off rose bushes in the mid-day heat in *Mansfield Park*. The ladies' activities in the potting shed in Sanditon are, alas, an invention of her posthumous collaborator and not of Jane Austen herself.

Mary Wollstonecraft may also be considered one of the earliest post-industrial women writers who saw gardening as a practical and psychological solace for the middle-class woman's empty life. "Gardening, experimental philosophy, and literature," she wrote in *A Vindication of the Rights of Woman* (1792), "would afford them [women in the middle rank of life] subjects to think of and matter for conversation, that in some degree would exercise their understanding."[56]

Wollstonecraft's suggestion was reiterated by women writers in a variety of gardening literature. Maria Elizabeth Jackson wanted to develop women's interest in botany more deeply and practically. In 1797, she produced *Botanical Dialogues between Hortensia and her Four Children*, which, revised in 1804, appeared as *Botanical Lectures by a Lady.* In *Sketches of the Physiology of Vegetable Life* (1811), Jackson wrote: "The taste for botany which has of late years so generally prevailed mongst all ranks and ages of society and more peculiarly manifested itself in the younger part of the female sex, has long rendered me desirous to attempt to lead the more inquiring minds of those engaged in this interesting and rational pursuit, to a deeper investigation..."[57] In 1816, Jackson published *The Florists Manual or Hints for the Construction of a Gay Flower Garden.* This was brought out in new editions in 1822 and 1827.

In 1823, Elizabeth Kent, a sister-in-law of Leigh Hunt, wrote *Flora Domestica, or the Portable Flower Garden.*[58] This treatise on potted plants addressed especially to those who lived in the city, was re-printed in 1826 and again in 1831. Kent's other work, *Sylvan Sketches; or, A Companion to the Park and the Shrubbery* (1825), is a four-hundred-page description of trees and shrubs interspersed with relevant poetry and designed for the type of young women so often evoked in Jane Austen's shrubberies.[69]

Maria Elizabeth Jackson, an Englishwoman, confirmed "the taste for botany... in the female sex," and wrote several books from 1811 onward hoping to develop female interest more deeply and more practically.

The maidens only ran into trouble with botany if they took it all too seriously. Professional botanists like John Lindley, formidable secretary of the London, later Royal Horticultural Society, very definitely did not want women sullying their premises. Members were elected and known as fellows. Guess what. Women could not become fellows until late in the nineteenth century and even then they were not fully vested. They were not invited to the society's dinners.

Agnes Ibbetson, 1757–1823, née Thomson, was a professional botanist in all but name yet was constantly rebuffed. In one of the prefaces to a paper, she recognized the enormous effrontery of what she was doing, presuming to tell men what to do. She had fully internalized what was expected of a woman but she did not back off. Ibbetson did have quite a lot of her work published in her lifetime, probably more than any other woman scientist of the era. The final book she was working on when she died was never published but the manuscript is in the library of the Natural History Museum in London.

Left a widow at the age of thirty-five, she moved to Exmouth in Devonshire to be close to her sister and took up her studies some years later. Ibbetson understood the value of close observation and noticed a great many aspects of plants in fine detail, hitherto unknown. She used a microscope very effectively. In thirteen years she produced fifty papers. She also did active experimental work to improve agricultural crops and was grudgingly admitted to membership in the Bath and West of England Society on the strength of her work. The society promoted scientific agriculture. A man who had done all this serious work would have been fêted.

Her contemporary, Thomas Andrew Knight of Herefordshire (1759–1838), worked in a similar vein. He came close to matching Gregor Mendel with his physiological studies of plant reproduction. The only reason that Mendel became immortal and Knight remained simply a very able horticulturist was that Mendel counted the results of his crosses and drew significant conclusions from them. Knight was deservedly elected president of the then London Horticultural Society (now Royal Horticultural Society) and held the post for almost thirty years. He too paid attention to significant detail. It is tempting to speculate how he and Mrs Ibbetson would have got on but traveling between Devonshire and Herefordshire was a huge undertaking at the time and I doubt they had any opportunity to meet.

One young Victorian single woman took her work in botany very seriously indeed. She lived in London but spent the summers in the Yorkshire countryside.[116] Her parents were the classic selfish and repressive Victorians who insisted that her place as a spinster was with them, in many ways like a slave. The pursuit of plants gave her a little freedom, though her mother upbraided her for taking time away from the dutiful round of social calls and her father was annoyed because she occasionally failed to bring him his slippers or prepare his cigars. Drawing and painting were her favorite activities but she was extremely observant and made a number of original observations about fungi and their cousins, the lichens. A neighbor in Yorkshire sent her every specimen he could find for her to draw.

She was the first person to identify the fact that lichens are actually a symbiotic mixture of fungi and algae and wrote a very well-reasoned paper with painstaking illustrations to prove her point. One of her uncles was well connected in the science world and he introduced her to one of his colleagues at Kew. Even with this entrée, her work was sidelined. There was no way she could read it herself at a meeting of the Linnean Society, but had to rely on a man to present it unenthusiastically in April 1897.

By the time anyone noticed what she had done, Beatrix Potter had moved on.

So far, no direct link between botany and gardening by women can be seen. This could be generational. Young ladies played at botany. More mature women gardened as well as appreciated botany. Gardening met many needs which will be examined in another chapter but at a very basic level, gardening necessitated getting dirty. Vain, pretty young girls did not want to do that.

The development of women's gardening theory and practice during the nineteenth century must also be considered as a reaction to the physical and psychological changes that transformed English towns and conditions of life in the wake of the industrial revolution.

Victorian observers were much exercised by the horrors of back-to-back cottages, the high density of unskilled labourers' dwellings, the smells of nonexistent plumbing, of dyeworks, of gasworks and of tanneries. In *The Condition of the Working Class in England* (1844), Engels described the squalor of thousands of laborers living in Manchester cellars and in her novel *North and South* (1853) Mrs. Gaskell incorporated details of this squalor in her characters' lives. Similar evidence has been amassed from Leeds, Glasgow, Liverpool and London.

As part of their charitable activities, middle-class women were anxious to improve the laborers' grim conditions of urban living. Elizabeth Gaskell visited factory workers in their miserable cellars and windowless and gardenless dwellings. As a reaction, underlying her need for personal refreshment and her great longing for the countryside of her youth, her own garden became of special importance. "A whispering of leaves and perfume of flowers always pervades her room," Charlotte Bronte wrote, describing a visit to the Gaskells' Manchester house.[61] Elizabeth Gaskell's youth in the country town of Knutsford, the model for her story *Cranford,* gave her gardening experience on which to base her Manchester planting in the late 1840s and 50s.

The manuals and guidebooks on gardening for ladies by Elizabeth Kent, Jane Loudon, and Louisa Johnson described above would serve women such as Gaskell, but perhaps even more importantly the women who had no country experience and no knowledge of the art.

By the end of her life, Elizabeth Gaskell had moved to a spacious house on the edge of Manchester, the third move in trying to escape the industrial smoke. Skilled laborers and artisans would live in houses less spacious yet more comfortable than the back-to-back dwellings and cellars of the unskilled laborers and immigrants. The houses of the skilled laborer and lower middle-class white collar workers offered small backyards which might be planted as gardens. It is these types of dwellings that contrast England so effectively with the housing of workers on the European continent, who lived in tenements without the freedom offered to the individual family by the individual garden. Presumably, the women inhabiting such houses with small gardens were those middle-class women in the Victorian Home who managed on £100–£300 a year, described by Branca in *Silent Sisterhood.*[86] Louisa Johnson addressed *Every Lady her Own Flower Gardener* to the "Industrious and Economical Only," and indeed, the "Silent Sisterhood" were nothing if not industrious and economical by necessity.

The link between gardening as a release and respite for

respectable married (and harried) women and its becoming a profession at which they excelled is to be found in the last quarter of the nineteenth century, aided by a variety of circumstances. The change came about as other aspects of women's lives were being questioned. With enough intelligent women asking questions and discussing their situation with each other, it became possible to envision a life beyond the household, even if one were married with children.

The largest question confronting serious women was the vote and the ability to help determine their own futures through politics and new laws. Laws governing women's rights were nonexistent. Women had no rights. A woman could not hold on to any money she had inherited. It automatically went to her husband. If she left her husband, the children remained with him. She could not take them with her. This situation had its own ironies. Maybe one or more of the children were not in fact the husband's.

Only when they could affect their condition through legislative means would women ever be released from this bondage. Married women had massive legal disabilities holding them in subjection. An heiress's money was her husband's to gamble away if he chose, leaving her with nothing. Everything belonged to a man.

The American Married Women's Property Act of 1848 was the first major advance in breaking that stranglehold. A similar act was not adopted until 1870 in the United Kingdom. This coincided with the new practice of impoverished English aristocrats marrying American heiresses to restore their family's coffers. What a pity for them if their noble husband squandered every penny of their dowry.

. . .

Tolstoy's *Anna Karenina* is a poignant reminder of what happens when a woman cannot see her child.[147] The possibility of greater freedom of action derived from overcoming that primary hurdle. They had to be considered to be mature adults for this to happen. Women had to throw off the canard of their allegedly weak brains and inability to make important decisions. The standard argument against allowing them to vote was that they would naturally share their husbands' s opinions on political questions, so what was the point! The nerve of them having their own independent opinions was unthinkable.

In colonial times, American women had been allowed to vote. Kentucky allowed women to vote in local elections if they were the head of a household in rural districts. By the end of the eighteenth century, however, whatever voting rights they had had were stripped from them, one state at a time.

For more than eighty years, women struggled to be allowed to vote, most notably in the United Kingdom and the United States. The continent of Europe was much more sluggish. Switzerland only gave women the vote in 1971. Curiously, the first places to allow women to vote were in the Rocky Mountain States in the Western United States, starting with the Territory of Wyoming in 1869. California followed soon after. Those women managed to do this without resorting to the startling tactics used in England. The eminent writer Louisa May Alcott was one of the very first women to register to vote in Massachusetts.

The English suffragettes invented terrorism to further their cause. They damaged public buildings and chained themselves to the fences at Westminster but the most shocking episode was the suicide at the Derby in 1913. Emily Wilding Davis deliberately threw herself under the hooves of a galloping horse at Epsom Downs, shouting "Votes for women." It required intense fanaticism to carry this out and enough women were prepared to die to create change that it worked. This background ferment allowed women to move from an occupation like gentle domestic gardening to considering a career as a professional gardener or even as a landscape architect if she were so inclined. Each woman was slowly becoming an individual in her own right and not merely an appendage of a man.

Once again, one needs to remember we are discussing married bourgeois women. Lively unconventional women had been singers, dancers, writers and actors all during this time oblivious to their social standing. When Mary Ann Evans moved in with George Lewes without marrying him, she lost all her social status but became famous as George Eliot. Such women did not rely on the approval of the ladies in their community for success.

Those other ladies had to juggle respectability with the ambition to improve their collective status. The lucky ones had a sympathetic husband. Both in the United Kingdom and the United States there were passionate male suffragists who supported these ambitions. In London, John Stuart Mill was one such man and in Washington DC the former slave Frederick Douglass was another.

4

GARDENING AS LIBERATION

Starting with the most superficial aspect of this new activity, what clothes did a woman who wanted to work in her garden wear? The idea that that there had to be specialized garments for different middle-class activities arose later in the nineteenth century. Men began to wear white to play cricket, largely because the light color kept them a bit cooler in the hot sun. The same held true for lawn tennis when it started. For poor people this was not even a question. They worked in whatever clothes they owned, other than their Sunday best.

In the drawings and early photographs which survive, ladies are seen outdoors in the highly unsuitable clothes they had to wear all the time: tight-waisted, long-skirted and heavy with shifts and petticoats. Keeping one's person and clothing clean in an era when there was no running hot water was a difficult task. Even the most highborn ethereal lady has sweat glands. The hems of the dresses trailed in the mud. Wearing an apron, as Gertrude Jekyll did, was a help but was only a partial solution.

When Sir William Thiselton-Dyer, director of Kew after his father in law Sir Joseph Hooker died, very reluctantly accepted women as professional gardeners in 1896, he insisted they wear brown woolen knickers. This made them look very much like the men, a radical departure for the age. Word about this spread and trainloads of salacious men would go to Kew to ogle the women doing their jobs.

The first women gardeners at Kew were Annie Gulvin, Alice Hutchings, Gertrude Cope, and Eleanor Morland. They had trained together at Swanley Horticultural College. The women worked twelve hours a day in the summer months, from 6 am to 6 pm. What is interesting is that they received the same (low) wages as the men. In the evenings they were expected to attend lectures about horticulture and to study very hard to get ahead. Alice Hutchings did become a sub foreman.

Slowly they started to drift away, some by marrying and others by finding better jobs. When the First World War began depleting the nation of men, they returned. Women gardeners became essential to the survival of public gardens and parks. At the Royal Botanic Gardens, Kew, twenty four of the thirty eight gardener positions were held by women in 1915. Three were foremen in 1916.

In the United States, John McLaren, supreme tyrant of the Golden Gate Park in San Francisco for forty-seven years, did not hire his first professional woman gardener until 1929. Sydney Stein Rich, nee Sadie Friedman, 1906–1956, was a Jewish woman born in Russia who had immigrated with her family to Brooklyn and then moved west to California. She was a graduate of the California School of

Gardening for Women in Hayward, now absorbed into Stanford University. The fees for her training were paid by the Sisterhood of Temple Emanu-El in San Francisco.

Mrs. Rich was very sensitive to the fact that she was the sole woman among a large number of men and dressed very conservatively to avoid being accused of flaunting her charms. She never wore shorts, even in the hottest weather. The other gardeners were very fond of her. She took a lot of trouble to help them prepare for examinations so they could win promotion. Few of them had had the benefit of her formal training in horticulture and did not even know the proper names of the plants they tended. Eventually, she was given full charge of the grounds and nursery as foreman. One of her responsibilities was to prepare the elaborate, very kitschy floral displays that punctuated the seasons. She died of malignant hypertension at the early age of fifty, a disorder which could be prevented now or if it occurred, treated successfully. Sydney Stein Rich's stepson recently died in 2020.

The schools for women gardeners adopted a variety of uniforms to give them a professional look. By World War I, women working on the land in the United Kingdom, the Women's Land Army, immortalized by D.H. Lawrence in his novella *The Fox*, replaced the farm laborers who had been conscripted.[115] They wore fully masculine clothes with knee breeches, long stockings, heavy boots, and woolen shirts.

The sartorial freedom was in itself one of the engines of change. It gave them an identity and the confidence to persevere and delve more deeply into horticultural life. It was a badge of honor.

Before that, women were not expected to be professional

gardeners. One very effective and skilled French woman gardener was almost written out of the family's seed business. The venerable firm of seedsmen to the king, Vilmorin et Andrieux, was founded in Paris in late 1774 and has only very recently been taken over by a global conglomerate. The company remained in the same building in the quai de la Mégisserie all that time. An ambitious physician, Pierre-Victoire Vilmorin, married Claude Geoffroy, the daughter of the seedsman Geoffroy. The father had given his daughter a thorough education in his craft and she was the acknowledged expert behind the business. Pierre-Victoire was really only the front man. Claude did everything else. Very few people were aware of this. The only other time you hear about a woman in this family is in the early 20th century. Louise Vilmorin decided to become a poet and artist and liberated herself from the family business.

Susan Bell did not maintain that all upper- and middle-class women ceased to garden entirely, only that the trend, especially among the nouveaux riches and middle-class women in growing urban communities, veered away from physical labor. Free spirits among upper- and middle-class women who gardened still existed in the late 18th century.

Lady Eleanor Butler and Lady Sarah Ponsonby, daughters of Irish peers who had run away together and lived in a Welsh cottage at Llangollen, described their gardening in letters and Butler's journal.

"Rose at six....my Beloved and I went into the garden...sowed three sorts of cucumber seeds."

Dorothy Wordsworth's Journal comprising her years at Grasmere c. 1800 continually had many entries like "worked in the garden," "cut the shrubs," "sowed the scarlett beans about the house," "sowed flowers," "nailed up the honey suckle," interspersed with her breathtaking observations on garden and wildflowers. Queen Charlotte, wife of George III, distracted herself by planting little oaks and geraniums when her husband was seriously ill and dying in 1811.

By the mid-nineteenth century, generally speaking, middle-class women no longer automatically took part in making things grow. Ditties were sung about the idleness and social pretentions even of English farmers' wives and daughters, who occupied themselves with "accomplishments," aping their betters by studying music, drawing and sketching with unimpressive results instead of contributing to their families or to society.

One aspect of these accomplishments was not entirely frivolous. A crop of women artists emerged who concentrated on botanical and horticultural themes, illustrating treatises and flower books. This important subset of women artists most often came from the middle or upper middle classes rather than from farms. "Superior" farm misses eventually saw the light and married within their own class, sensibly moving on.

Back in the eighteenth century one of the outstanding examples of such artists was the Scotswoman Elizabeth Blackwell (1700–1758), the daughter of a successful merchant, whose husband Alexander, a physician and writer, also gardener to the Earl of Chandos at Canons, became bankrupt. She had to save her family from starvation and used her ability to paint flowers as the way to do it. She took lodgings near the Chelsea Physic Garden, the ground of the London Society of Apothecaries and offered to be their painter. In 1737, the society brought out a book, *A Curious Herbal,* with more than five hundred of Mrs. Blackwell's paintings and descriptions.[67] It ran into several editions and even a German translation issued by the great botanical publishing house Trew of Nurnberg.

Mary Delany (1700–1788), was another example of an artistic woman inspired by flowers. She was born into an aristocratic family and showed unusual talent even as a girl and young woman. At the age of 74 she began a unique pastime, making cutout paper flowers unlike anything ever seen before. These mosaics are so lifelike that botanists, like Sir Joseph Banks, the President of the Royal Society, were able to use them as workable models. She completed nine hundred and eighty-five specimens by the time she was 86 years old. Her great-niece bound them into ten volumes and presented them to the British Museum in 1897. This collection is now one of the prized exhibits of the Department of Prints and Drawings in the British Museum.

An early American botanist fitting into this category is Jane Colden (1724–1766), the daughter of the physician Cadwallader Colden in upstate New York. She was recognized by great botanists like William Bartram and Alexander Garden in America, the chief British botanists and Linnaeus himself.

In the eighteenth century a number of aristocratic Englishwomen learned flower painting from the outstanding German botanical artist Georg Ehret. In the nineteenth century, the Belgian Pierre-Joseph Redouté became not only the greatest botanical artist in France, but also the flower painter and art teacher to three successive Queens and Empresses: Marie Antoinette, the Empress Josephine, and her successor, Marie Louise. Redouté had been apprenticed to a well-known artist who specialized in great panoramas. When questioned about his skill with flowers, Redouté very pragmatically replied, "It is much quicker and easier to paint a flower than a thirty-foot canvas."

This type of activity among the foremost ladies of the land made an impression on parents of middle-class daughters and the teaching of art as well as botany was an essential part of the curriculum of young ladies' accomplishments around the turn of the 18th and 19th centuries. Throughout the nineteenth century, a number of women produced valuable artistic and botanical contributions as a result of these earlier influences. The English ones, Mrs. Cookson, Mrs. Robley, Mrs. Bury, Clara Maria Pope and Augusta Withers, come to mind but in spite of the fact that their work was essential to the botanical periodicals and treatises of this period, their names are buried. Only the male editors and publishers' names adorn these books.

One of the more startling examples of this practice is the illustration of the vegetation on which John Audubon's birds disport themselves. Many of these trees and flowers were painted by his good friend and admirer Maria Martin (1796–1863). The American Heritage Edition of the *Original Water Color Paintings of John James Audubon* identifies twenty of the habitats Maria Martin painted.[68] Other authors feel that she may have been responsible for all the vegetation in Volume Four of Audubon's *Birds of America*.

Maria Elizabeth Jackson, an Englishwoman, confirmed "the taste for botany... in the female sex," and wrote several books from 1811 onward hoping to develop female interest more deeply and more practically. By 1825, Elizabeth Kent wrote *Sylvan Sketches; or, A Companion to the Park and the Shrubbery.* Four hundred pages describing trees and shrubs were interspersed with relevant poetry, designed for the type of young ladies so often evoked in Jane Austen's novels. Two years earlier, in 1823, Elizabeth Kent, a sister in law of Leigh Hunt, had written on "portable Flower Gardens," that is, potted plants for those who lived in the city.[58]

By the mid-nineteenth century, there was, at least among middle- and upper-class English women, an increasing preoccupation with physical gardening. There is considerable evidence for this resurgence of women's interest in horticulture.

First, as noted above, books on gardening written by, and specifically for, women began to appear in increasing numbers. Secondly, women's diaries, letters, and memoirs describe gardening activities, expertise in Linnean botanical classification and an earlier interest in transplanting foreign or exotic plants into their own English gardens. Thirdly, women began to make names for themselves as landscape architects and designers and fourthly, they founded schools of horticulture specifically to train women as jobbing gardeners, market gardeners and head gardeners for large public and private establishments.

Barbara Charlton, who lived near Hexham in Northumberland, wrote in 1861: "I have been for some time collecting specimens of ferns to plant out in the woods, where they throve pretty well considering the climate. I had also tried to acclimatize violets, primroses and lilies of the valley in the sunny spots, but even so they refused to take life."

Juliana Ewing, following her new husband to his army duty in Fredericton, New Brunswick wrote home to her mother in England: "I have a wonderful lot of gardening on my shoulders ... I have to make my plans and arrange my crops for the kitchen garden as well as look after my own flower garden...it is a great enjoyment to me...." Further, she wrote to her sister: "You can hardly think how delicious it feels to garden after six months of frost and snow." In June she wrote: "My Jonquils are just coming out and one or two other things...I mean to plant scarlet runners to attract the humming birds." In another letter to her sister she wrote about the "soothing effect of nature" and I think the smell of earth and plants has a physical anodyne about it somehow! One cannot explain it." In a letter to a friend, she wrote in 1883: "My garden is a great joy to me. Even you, I think, would allow me a moderate amount of "grubbing" in between brain work."

Juliana Ewing was very ill for long periods of her life and died aged forty-four. In the year before her death, she and her husband moved to a new house in Somerset and she immersed herself in designing and planting a garden. She wrote to another gardening friend, the Rev. Goring: "Moreover by a superhuman – or anyhow superfrail feminine effort – last Saturday... I took up all that remained of the cabbage garden – spread heaps of ashes, marked out another path, made my new walk and edged it with broken tiles that came off the roof, when the strong winds blew – an economy which pleased me much. Thus, I am now entirely flower garden and with room for more flowers." In December, recovering from a severe bout of neuralgia, she was putting in rose bushes and wrote: "Fortunately the border was ready and well manured and I only had to dig holes in very soft stuff – but I am very weak."

Frances Waddington, an Englishwoman who married

the Baron Bunsen, a diplomat and future Prussian ambassador to London, wrote to her mother from Rome: "I have been often in the garden, having it put in order, and making a hedge, or rather reforming a hedge which I have replanted with roses, oleanders, calceolarias, and geraniums; it is not to be described how geraniums have flourished in the garden in the short time I have had it to myself – a set of slips put in in March have become almost trees in the course of the summer." After her return to England, she wrote to her son: "I am much struck with the luxury in garden cultivation that is everywhere seen in England, far different from poor Italy where everything might be in far greater perfection, were nature only a little assisted by industry."

Caroline Cornwallis writing to her mother from Italy also remarked on the lack of expertise of Italian gardeners when compared with English ones. She gathered Italian plants to bring back and transplant in her English garden: "I have been collecting flower roots very diligently," she wrote, "and shall have a good many pretty ones; amongst the rest a hepatica, of a colour I have never seen in England, a fine lilac..." The Baroness Bunsen also brought plants from Italy to England, as did Juliana Ewing from New Brunswick.

The letters of Mrs. Gaskell, published in their entirety, show just how important the "domestic details" were.[61] Elizabeth Gaskell was typical in some ways with her fragmented and wide-ranging activities, encompassing maternal, housekeeping and parish duties. She was unusual in that she also wrote many excellent novels often reflecting tragic contemporary social problems. She was a close friend of Charlotte Bronte and wrote the first biography of that astounding woman.

. . .

Mrs. Gaskell was obviously a gardener of the most committed kind, for she frequently slipped the odd gardening reference into her stream-of-consciousness correspondence. In May 1860, she wrote to her daughter Marianne: "It is hard work writing a novel all morning, spudding up dandelions all afternoon, and writing again at night. Moreover, I had a dreadful headache on Friday; was utterly kilt and incapable which came I suppose from going with Julia to the theatre on Thursday.... I am getting on with my book, 117 pages done of 570 at least; and I've broken my back over dandelions. And I have not got a cook."

Not having a cook was more than a minor inconvenience in that period. Before refrigeration, electricity, and running hot water, all food had to be purchased frequently and processed very laboriously by hand.

From Mary Wollstonecraft onwards, nineteenth-century women's writing on gardening shows that they thought of the art of gardening as an outlet for psychological and physical needs. They saw gardening as an answer not only to the human need for beauty but to their particular problems as women. Elizabeth Gaskell is one of the many Victorian women whose letters, diaries and memoirs refer to their work in the garden as a pleasurable and satisfying occupation. Upper and upper-middle class women who left records of this type were both unmarried, like those addressed by Louisa Johnson, and over-busy housewives like Gaskell herself. In 1851, Elizabeth Gaskell was invited to visit the Great Exhibition in London, and wrote to her friend, Eliza Fox: "Oh dear, how I should like to come....But my dear don't you see there are beds to be taken down and curtains dyed and carpets cleaned, and curtains chosen, and carpets selected and cabbages planted in our garden – and that I am the factotum della citta – and it's Figaro qua, Figaro la, all day long..."

In 1857, she wrote to Charles Eliot Norton at Harvard: "If I had a library like yours, all undisturbed for hours, how I would write! Mrs. Chapone's letters should be nothing to mine! I would outdo Rasselas in fiction. But you see every body comes to me perpetually. Now this hour since Breakfast I have had to decide on the following variety of important questions. Boiled beef – how long to boil? What perennials will do in Manchester smoke, and what colours our garden wants. Length of a skirt for a gown! Salary of a nursery governess..."

Other women showed an equal pride and delight in the work to be done in the garden. Mary Howitt, for example, wrote to her sister in 1837: "Our garden would of itself furnish us with employment, and it seems to me that it would be such a pure and heavenly life, especially if one at the same time wrote books that did the world good."[70]

Jane Carlyle wrote in 1850 to her cousin: "I have got to-day some slips of the sweet briar...which I wrote to Mrs. Russel for – the slips I got from the Garden at Haddington have taken root." Barbara Charlton, who lived near Hexham in Northumberland, wrote in 1861: "I have been for some time collecting specimens of ferns to plant out in the woods, where they throve pretty well considering the climate. I had also tried to acclimatize violets, primroses and lillies of the valley in the sunny spots, but even so they refused to take life."

According to Susan Bell, merely reading those portions of diaries and letters extracted for publication, however, is not the best evidence for gardening among Victorian women. Often the editor stated explicitly that only matters of "public interest" would be included, while the "purely domestic" details were to be omitted in the published works. Even so, the evidence of selected material from nineteenth-century editions shows that gardening was an integral part of a majority of upper- and upper-middle-class women's lives.

By the end of the century, two generations of domestic middle-class women gardeners and women writers on gardening had set the stage for professional women gardeners and landscape designers in the 20th century. This period coincided clearly with the entry of women into many other professional schools (medicine, art, academia generally), with the height of the suffrage movement, and yet again, with the concern over surplus of unmarried women.

Foreign observers, like the well-known American garden author Helena Rutherfurd Ely, specifically held up upper-class English women as an example to Americans by the end of Queen Victoria's reign. In 1903, she wrote that "nearly every great lady in England takes a personal interest in her gardens...and knows all about the plants and flowers, while in America the majority of women having large places leave the direction...to the gardener and thus miss a great and healthful pleasure."

The outstanding example of a professional landscape designer and gardener is Gertrude Jekyll (1843–1932). Jekyll is recognized by garden historians as an artist who revolutionized garden design at the end of the 19th century and who was a basic influence on gardeners and architects, both in England and in the United States. She visualized the importance of linking house and garden as a single unit. (See page 149)

5

SCHOOLS OF HORTICULTURE FOR WOMEN

Schools of horticulture or gardening for women arose to fill a social need. With so much of the work women had traditionally done being erased by industrial and commercial changes in the mid nineteenth century many women no longer had a role in a society for which marriage and motherhood were the sole arbiters of success. Before adequate methods of birth control large families with eight or more children were still the norm in all classes. If young unmarried women of the middle and upper middle classes had not found a husband in their first bloom of youth they resigned themselves to a life of unpaid service in the family. The really unfortunate ones were left alone, quite penniless if they did not even have this family network to shelter them.

They could not go out to work like a working class girl. They had to sit tight and nurse their chilblains in chilly rooms, unable to afford coal for an adequate fire. In the last quarter of the nineteenth century this set of women was referred both in Great Britain and on the continent of Europe to as "surplus". That era was alive with change. New recognition of social needs was yoked to the movement for a voice in their own destinies.

The realization that women collectively as a segment of society had serious disabilities that could be improved was a signal advance. Identifying a problem is the first step in ameliorating it. During the heady period when women were starting to think about having rights for themselves, not just as accessories to a husband, a few paid attention to the large army of unmarried women who were immured in insensitive families, used as unpaid servants to take care of children or sick relatives. Active and somewhat rebellious women believed that women should be able to exercise a profession and make their own living if they chose.

Childless women lived longer than women who had borne children. Male and female mortality rates varied by social class and marital status. Longevity was affected by the basic natural functions. The principal killer of women was childbirth. Unmarried women did not face those hazards and lived longer. This survival was part of the reason single women presented a challenge.

Every family had its maiden aunts, its spinster sisters and solitary cousins. W. S. Gilbert immortalized this situation with "... and we are his sisters and his cousins and his aunts , his sisters and his cousins and his aunts" in *The Mikado*. At a time of very large families an over supply of women was inevitable.

No one talked of surplus men in this context. There was some sort of place for all men in society whatever their gifts or lack thereof. The capacity for a woman to earn a living in a respectable yet satisfying fashion needed to become a reality. Formal education seemed to be the best approach. Some outstanding women who were driven, like Beatrix Jones Farrand, took matters into their own hands and found mentors to guide them. Less fortunate women required help and leaders of the nascent women's movement believed this was the way to go.

Schools of gardening opened at about the same time as much better formal education for girls was being created. Girls education outside the home had been a very haphazard affair throughout the nineteenth century, ranging from the highly superficial institutions for teaching social graces to grim penitentiaries like Lowood in *Jane Eyre*. Thank to pioneers like Miss Beal and Miss Buss of Cheltenham Ladies College, middle class girls could now learn the same curriculum as their brothers with classics, literature, history, mathematics and science all taught to a very high standard. Both boarding schools and day schools opened at roughly the same time, sponsored by thoughtful men who realized this was what was needed.

At about the same time two different independent women of means in England hit on the same idea, to build on women's known enjoyment of gardening to make it a source of livelihood. Fulfilling the need for self-expression and making something new leads to considerable intellectual and aesthetic satisfaction. In western civilization, men have, with varying fluctuations, had far greater opportunities for doing just this. For women, maternal and domestic tasks have often consumed most of their time and energy. About the only thing middle-class and upper-middle-class women were expected to do outside the home was to participate in some decorous charity work and instill religion into their children. Thus, within the confines of women's domestic pursuits, gardening provided an attractive outlet for women hemmed in by duty.

Throughout the nineteenth century, women writers on gardening were interested in designing gardens suited to a more human scale, as befitted a new suburban spread and the development of an extended middle class. They were equally concerned with opportunities for women's self-expression. In addition, although Gertrude Jekyll wrote that the garden "should never be large enough to be tiring," it provided much needed physical exercise, especially for "ladies" whose position in society forbade other physical work. Louisa Johnson, writing in 1840, spoke of gardening "bracing the system by its healthful tendency," and Frances Wolseley in 1900 cited physicians' recommendations of gardening to combat disease and lack of exercise.

Finally, along with exercise, self-expression, and the development of practical skills, work in the garden offered women emotional peace. Whether the gardener be the cottage woman from whom Gertrude Jekyll drew her inspiration; the heartsick Queen Charlotte; the harassed author Elizabeth Gaskell, wife of a busy vicar in a poor district of an ugly industrial city; the disappointed spinster evoked by Louisa Johnson or the "surplus woman" of concern to the Countess of Warwick, their problems were alleviated or prevented by the need to maintain their precious gardens.

Two twentieth-century women writers, one American, one English, have immortalized the garden as an emotional refuge: May Sarton and Vita Sackville-West. May Sarton was the daughter of George Sarton, a well-known scholar of the history of science but a somewhat emotionally withdrawn human being, not the best person to be a father.

May Sarton's *Journal of a Solitude* (1973) is a convincing statement of the physical effort required and the equilibrium gained by the steady but creative routine of the gardening year.[73] Sarton's greatest contribution is her struggle to distinguish between the delight of solitude and the hell of loneliness. A very fine line exists between them and one which Sarton brings out in her *Journal*.

Her great comfort and steady resource was the garden. Here are two excerpts describing her mood. "This morning I woke at four and lay awake for an hour or so in a bad state. It is raining again. I got up finally and went about the daily chores, waiting for the sense of doom to lift and what did it was watering the house plants. Suddenly joy came back, because I was fulfilling a simple need, a living one. Dusting never has that effect.... Whatever peace I know rests in the natural world, in feeling myself part of it," and

"Then I went out for two hours late in the afternoon and put in a hundred tulips. In itself that would not be a big job, but everywhere I have to clear space for them, weed, divide perennials, rescue iris that is being choked by violets. I really get to weeding only in the spring and autumn, so I am working through a jungle now. Doing it I feel strenuously happy and at peace. At the end of an afternoon on a gray day, the light is sad and one feels the chill, but the bitter smell of earth is a tonic."

Sarton was an admirer of one of the greatest women gardeners, Victoria Sackville-West, who is remembered for her complex personal life and her writing but mostly for the legacy of her garden designs. She wrote about her work in the garden and her plants in newspapers and magazines every week for many years. The public was always enchanted with her garden writings.

Frances Wolseley expressed herself on freedom and emotional satisfaction: "Perhaps if she is a governess or companion she may live in the country and have all these pleasures of cowslips in the meadows and the fresh sweet scents but will she fully relish them if she has no freedom?" and "We see daily before us leisured women who from lack of pleasant, wholesome interests and bodily exercise without scope for reasonable aspirations, have become anaemic parodies of the sex. The insidious malady... masquerades under the old-fashioned term "ennui" or the new fangled names of nervous exhaustion, break-down, overwork, hysteria, decadence. I believe I am justified in saying that medical men, who can appreciate the often aimless, humdrum existence of many women of the wealthier classes and the debility of those in our large towns, find in gardening a good agent for their relief."

SCHOOLS OF GARDENING FOR LADIES

The evolution from "domestic" to "professional" gardening for women was thus more than a matter of change from cultivating one's own garden to cultivating someone else's garden as a paid professional. It was a formidable change in what was proper for a lady. The development of women's horticultural schools in the late 19th and early 20th century played a central role in this change, producing competent women gardeners who were employed throughout the western world.

During the late 19th century, middle-class English women entered professional gardening through a gradual evolution from domestic amateurism. Two English schools, the Glynde School for Lady Gardeners in Sussex, and the

Studley Horticultural College at Studley Castle in Warwickshire, were founded by aristocratic women, the Viscountess Wolseley and the Countess of Warwick. One of their expressed purposes was to create a respectable profession for "surplus women," a profession, moreover, that combined earning power with freedom and emotional satisfaction.

Sensing a serious need, both worked tirelessly to get women enrolled in schools of horticulture in the United Kingdom. These strongminded women of means were in the forefront of women's liberation, the modern term for what they were doing. Even before the slaughter of World War I, millions of well-brought-up English women were unable to marry for lack of a dowry. Training them for a solid livelihood was a lifesaver for them, offering dignity and social acceptance. The Countess of Warwick specifically concerned herself with "surplus women" (her term).

Frances Wolseley described the requirements and aims for her pupils at Glynde and at the other schools in *Gardening for Women* (1908). Her objective with this book was to make gardening a respectable profession for upper- and upper-middle-class women, as well as to persuade employers and male under-gardeners to accept women as professional garden supervisors. The book stressed the innate "taste" and refinement which apparently came naturally to a "lady" gardener and which would therefore make her a suitable candidate for the profession.

This approach would overcome objections of parents whose daughters wanted to become gardeners and would appeal to employers having problems with head gardeners lacking in taste. The scientific knowledge of the professional "lady gardener" would make her capable of supervising the untrained but possibly obstreperous male. In addition, the new head "lady gardener" should dismiss the first drunken under-gardener she meets. There was ample precedent for this bold step, with the Ladies of Llangollen for example. In spite of their unusual choices they were still the daughters of aristocrats and did not hesitate to dismiss an insolent man who drank on the job.

Wolseley's book also gave very practical advice on tools, dress, habits, and manners to be cultivated by ladies who planned to follow gardening as a profession. Wet gloves and poor shoes produce chilblains; leggings must be of leather, not of cloth. Cloth is too porous and hard to clean. Floppy hats are out. Caps are in. Students were expected to carry out the most menial tasks, work a full week of long hours, and be as knowledgeable about basic practical details as about the scientific composition of the soil.

Not only was the lady gardener sanctioned by women like Viscountess Wolseley and the Countess of Warwick to work for pay, she was also allowed to dirty her hands. Jane Loudon writing her domestic *Gardening for Ladies* in 1840 had insisted that gloves be worn for gardening. Almost seventy years later, Frances Wolseley wrote tartly that certain work cannot be done in gloves; after all, "hands will wash."

One scholar has counted nineteen private schools of gardening for women in England before the Second World War.[132] A few of them were quite small and ephemeral, only lasting a few years at most. They were the personal businesses of an individual woman and if that woman retired the school closed. The descriptions which follow are principally of the more substantial schools. In general, they chose to adhere to higher academic standards and seek certification from authorized bodies like the Royal Horticultural Society (RHS).

The RHS laid out both theoretical and practical requirements for certification. A thorough and detailed knowledge of botany was basic. Students also had to know some general physics and chemistry. The curriculum covered soils, plant physiology such as seed germination and growth, with its dependence on water, temperature and air circulation, other methods of vegetal reproduction, development of flowers and fruit, nomenclature and details of proper cultivation. The practical aspects of the courses put much of this into action. Students had to know how to choose the best site to grow certain crops, how to measure and prepare the site, which tools to use, how to fertilize the soil, how to prevent or at least minimize the damage due to pests and how to propagate seedlings for an adequate crop. The schools also catered mainly to women who had already had some higher education and access to means. Having dirty hands did not mean they were no longer ladies.

The English schools were part of an international development in the late 19th century. Wolseley described some twenty existing Western European schools in 1907. Students from as far afield as the United States and Russia attended the famous school of Pomology and Horticulture for Women at Marienfelde near Berlin. In the United States, numerous coeducational colleges offered training in horticulture (for example, the New York State College of Agriculture at Cornell University). The Missouri Botanical Garden at St. Louis, Missouri, affiliated with Washington University, offered practical and theoretical gardening to men and women, though scholarships were only available to men. A private school was projected in Cheltenham,

Pennsylvania to be known as the Pennsylvania School of Horticulture for Women, and another, the Lowthorpe School for Lady Gardeners at Groton, Massachusetts, concentrating on landscape design, was founded by Mrs. Low in 1900. E. S. Graves, Director of the Yale University Forest School, had high praise for Mrs. Low's School for Lady Gardeners after it had been in existence for seven years. He considered it the only school where women could secure an adequate training in landscape gardening and offered his services and assistance.

Two American women landscape designers who had an international reputation by 1907 were Elizabeth Lee of Philadelphia and Beatrix Jones (later better known as Beatrix Farrand) of New York, a niece of Edith Wharton. Farrand published an important article on the philosophy of landscape design in *Scribner's Magazine* in 1907. Later, she designed the gardens at Dumbarton Oaks, as well as gardens at Yale University and part of the White House grounds. Farrand also designed the grounds for the famous private opera house at Glyndebourne in England.

Rigorous training in horticulture meant that women could take on serious responsibilities previously restricted to men for gardens and estates. In many instances, the men had only been apprenticed to head gardeners but it was gradually becoming necessary for them to study a fixed curriculum before going on to the practicum. The remarkable women who led the movement in horticultural education believed in this aspect of training. It underscored just how serious they were, developing an *esprit de corps* among the trainees and graduates. They were at pains to show there was nothing frivolous about their efforts, no frilly sunbonnets or gauzy shawls.

The redoubtable Miss Havergal of the Waterperry school, the stately woman who ran the school for many years, refused to allow even the tiniest young woman to use a smaller set of tools. This was confirmed by the daughter in law of one of those students, Gillian Mawrey. Her husband's mother Alice had been a pupil at Waterperry and was barely five feet tall, but Miss Havergal stood firm. Everything had to be done strenuously and in the right way, the same way as the men.

The well-known English gardener and photographer Valerie Finnis was an exemplar of this philosophy.[90] This was the life she wanted. She voluntarily submitted herself to a rigid external discipline when she could have chosen to leave for a softer life. Valerie Finnis spent almost her entire adult life at Waterperry College under the revered Miss Havergal. Even after graduation, Miss Finnis stayed on as a teacher, still wearing the uniform. In late middle life, she moved to a house of her own and devoted herself to its garden, planting many rare species not often seen. The garden was so beautiful that charities begged her to allow the public to visit it as a way to raise money.

On one such occasion, Miss Finnis overheard an elderly man commenting on these plants, naming them correctly. She heard him say: "By God, she's got a *Gillenia trifoliata.*" This was the first time she had ever come across someone who knew about her treasures. She rushed over to talk to him. They became friends and before long they married. Miss Finnis was over fifty and Sir David Scott was a widower much older than she was with one son. They spent the honeymoon on their knees, weeding.

The fee structure of these specialized schools indicates that the students still had to be "ladies." The daughter of an estate laborer or a local cook would not be able to find that much money every year. There are records of gardeners' sons following in their fathers' footsteps but only a very few of their daughters. Saving up to buy a typewriter and take a few lessons was more within their reach. The tradition of having women come in to do the weeding on a large estate persisted down into the nineteenth century, but that did not translate into many such women deciding to become gardeners themselves. Weeding was simply a low level skill and a way to augment the very meagre family earnings.

Did this solution to the problem work, creating special schools for women who wanted to be gardeners? There was no question that graduates of such schools were well trained and capable. Stepping back and looking at the numbers involved shows that the endeavor could come under the rubric of "boutique" solution. Using a set of conservative assumptions fewer than ten or fifteen thousand such gardeners eventually emerged from the aggregate efforts of the schools. Many schools could only accept ten students. Larger ones could accept perhaps thirty.

Making the assumption that there were about twenty five schools throughout Great Britain, every year between five hundred and six hundred young women would be enrolled. This meant that in a decade up to six thousand graduates could be expected. Three decades might produce up to fifteen or eighteen thousand graduates.

· · ·

Gradually the idea of professional women gardeners became less radical. Most of the schools had disappeared after thirty years, their work absorbed by large formal programs and merged with colleges and universities. In reality the projected number of graduates is an overestimate as many left the schools for various reasons without graduating. A student became ill because of the harsh conditions, courses might be too difficult or their financial support dried up.

We are left thinking that this was a very good idea but on far too small a scale to solve the huge problem the organizers confronted. One of the principal problems was the huge ratio of teachers to students. There was no "economy of scale" and few short cuts. Compared to the force exerted on women's freedom by the arrival of the bicycle and typewriter this was a drop in the bucket.

THE ENGLISH FOUNDERS

Frances Garnet, 2nd Viscountess Wolseley, 1872–1936, was the only child of Sir Garnet Joseph Wolseley, 1st Viscount Wolseley, chief of the armed services in the United Kingdom. He was given the title in recognition of his work. Even though Frances was a woman she quite unusually inherited the title after he died. Frances Wolseley never married or had children, so the title went into abeyance on her death.

She never wanted to be a conventional woman of the epoch. Frances Wolseley was presented at court but decided she did not want to marry and devoted herself to the betterment of women's lives through horticultural education. By the time she was twenty-seven, an advanced age for young women of the day, she was devoting herself to country pursuits and her dogs.

Lady Wolseley opened her school in 1902 and later moved it to larger premises. At first she was involved very closely with its day-to-day affairs but after some time detached herself to work on the larger aspects of this movement. She wrote several important books, including *Women in Agriculture*, a compendium of ways in which market gardens and other enterprises could be successfully run by women.

COUNTESS WARWICK

Frances Evelyn Maynard, known as "Daisy," 1861–1938, inherited very large fortunes from both her father and grandfather at the age of three, providing an income of £30,000 per annum, an astronomical sum back then. When she married Lord Brooke, who became the Earl of Warwick, this money was combined with that of her husband, also a very wealthy man.

At first she used the money to enjoy herself, throwing extravagant parties and disporting herself with men like the Prince of Wales. Contemporary portraits show her to be a very lovely young woman. She also wanted to create beautiful gardens and displayed her skill at the family estate at Easton in Essex.

A severe public scolding by Robert Blatchford, the editor of the Socialist newspaper *The Clarion*, about her wastefulness and how the money used for such a party could have fed hundreds of poor people or helped to educate some of them in the 1890s opened her eyes. She had naively thought that the classic "trickle down" system would help to alleviate poverty in her area. It is eternally to her credit that she took the criticism to heart and mended her ways. Countess Warwick became a card-carrying Socialist and thus an enemy of her class.

In a strange echo of Ellen Willmott's fate, she too ended up quite poor but for different reasons. The bulk of her income came from the products of her lands. When the agricultural depression hit in 1893 and lasted for several years, her income dropped sharply. Huge quantities of grain from Ukraine and Canada were a glut on the market, driving down prices. She also spent very freely but not as wantonly as Miss Willmott. She used her money to benefit others less fortunate than she was. Her younger son only inherited the rather paltry sum of £37,000 when she died.

Apart from the schools she founded, Countess Warwick also campaigned endlessly for other social improvements. Life in late Victorian Britain was a Darwinian struggle. Public education for the masses had begun to emerge as an important matter in the 1860s, culminating in the Education Act of 1870. It was highly imperfect but it was a start. The Church of England had fought a bitter rearguard battle to maintain its monopoly over primary education but did not have the resources or burning passion to reach every eligible child it should.

Enlightened municipalities took up the cause. Adult education was championed by groups like the Fabians as well as many charities. Gardening and horticulture were only among the many other practical evening and night classes sponsored by entities like the London County Council. Countess Warwick responded by opening a school of fine needlework, a traditional female skill, before coming up with the idea of a school of gardening. Edith Wharton, a noted gardener as well as author, had done something similar for destitute French girls during the First World War, offering them shelter, a refuge and way to earn a living by sewing and embroidery.

PRIVATE HORTICULTURAL SCHOOLS AND COLLEGES FOR LADY GARDENERS

ALDERSEY HALL
Near Chester, Cheshire

Miss Ruth Wheeler had started a nursery at Cosham near Portsmouth in Hampshire in 1902 but in 1916 moved it to Cheshire. She was a graduate of Lady Warwick's school at Studley and used a gift of £1000 from her father to create the business. By 1904, she was taking in students who paid a guinea a week for tuition and board. Even though Ruth left to get married in about 1908, her other sisters, Laura, Sylvia, and Amy, stepped in and kept the school going. Laura was the principal and Amy did the housekeeping. They were very serious about it, with many students gaining certificates from the Royal Horticultural Society.

In 1907 the nursery was providing sixty-five hampers of produce a week and also ten to twelve hours of jobbing gardening. In 1913, the school advertised in a trade magazine that they could take ten students at year at £60 per annum. By moving to the larger premises in Cheshire, they could broaden the curriculum, adding more agriculturally based subjects like poultry rearing and dairy work. With the First World War in full swing, all farmers were charged with producing more food. A world-famous breeder of sweet peas in Worcestershire, Hilda Hemus, had to plough up her flowers and plant wheat. In spite of the emphasis on academic performance, very few records survive of this school.

INSTRUCTION IN PRACTICAL GARDENING FOR LADIES
Glynde, near Lewes, Sussex
Principal: The Hon. Frances Wolseley

Lady Wolseley founded her school in 1901. She very prudently requested the most famous horticulturists of the day to be patrons: William Robinson, Ellen Willmott and Gertrude Jekyll, thus giving the school an aura of glamour and professional skill from the start. The irony was that Miss Willmott would never let a woman gardener anywhere near her properties.

Viscountess Wolseley had been born in London and moved very frequently with her father's postings. They eventually settled in Sussex. She became very concerned about agricultural reform and used her own home to start the school. Lady Wolseley later moved it to larger premises nearby. Perhaps because she came from a military family, this school had stricter discipline than some of the others. Students wore a uniform and worked very hard every day with few breaks. They were punished for infractions of the rules and rewarded with medals for good behavior.

The school had a more broadly based curriculum than Thatcham, with more classes in horticultural theory taught by noted male experts. The students lived out at a cost of 17 shillings a week. They paid £20 per annum for instruction and were charged extra for the specialty classes and being prepared to take the RHS examinations. The curriculum was based on a two-year course but it was possible only to stay for one year. If a student had to be expelled the fees were refunded.

In spite of Lady Wolseley's careful planning, the RHS was not ready to accept women gardeners. Very few Glynde candidates were allowed to sit for the examinations and so could not obtain the credential. They were still too far ahead of their time.

World War I made the difference. There were simply not enough men left to be gardeners. Many of the other ranks had been gardeners. When they departed, their employers had few choices. In many cases the employers themselves were officers and were called back to serve or had joined up. Almost all adult men were in the armed forces and the condition of residential gardens was an afterthought. Most gardens were left untended. Only a few landowners thought of hiring women gardeners and in any event, women who could work the soil were required in agriculture to grow urgently needed food. Midway through the war German prisoners of war became available but were still largely used in agriculture.

THE HORTICULTURAL COLLEGE AT SWANLEY
Swanley, Kent

The Horticultural College at Swanley founded for men in 1889 opened its doors to the first women students in 1891. By 1907 the student body was exclusively female. Miss F. Wilkinson was the Principal. John Lawson was the head gardener. Swanley is in Kent, near Chatham, seventeen miles from London. The estate had more than forty acres of land with which to teach the classes.

The school was extremely professional with two or three-year curricula in horticulture, botany, soil chemistry, and related scientific subjects. There was a broad range of study, all taught by experts in the field. The fees were quite a bit higher, up to £96 a year for a student who wanted a larger set of rooms. Swanley's students did well in the RHS examinations and managed to find good positions as head gardeners of large public or private establishments, as market gardeners, or as teachers of nature study.

Viscountess Wolseley listed some statistics in 1908:

Twenty six graduates became head gardeners, twenty five were market gardeners, twenty three were teachers, nine were jobbing gardeners, three took up landscape architecture and a small number went into other specialties. This was an impressive result.

She also reported on their success in the national examinations. The colleges entered sixteen women for the RHS examinations in April 1907, competing with a total of 142 candidates. Eight obtained first class honors, six second class and two third class. Here too was an impressive result. One young woman who did not complete the course but who went on to a distinguished career in flower breeding was Isabella Preston. She became world famous for her work with lilies and lilac. (See page 196)

STUDLEY HORTICULTURAL COLLEGE
Studley, Warwickshire

The Countess of Warwick set up Studley Horticultural

College at her own estate in Warwickshire not too far from Birmingham. This school offered all the important courses required for success in the RHS examinations, as well as other useful subjects like bookkeeping, beekeeping, cooking, jam making, and preserving fruit. The countess employed qualified teachers in botany and horticulture but also encouraged her students to study farming techniques. The students were expected to enroll for the two-year program. If a young woman elected to live in a small cubicle at the college the fees were £80 but if she wanted a study bedroom they rose to £120 per year.

A graduate of Studley, Judith Walrond-Skinner, opened her own school in Hayward, California, in 1924. The California School of Gardening for Women survived about ten years before being merged with Stanford University.

THE THATCHAM FRUIT AND FLOWER FARM AND SCHOOL OF GARDENING
Henwick, Berkshire

The Thatcham Fruit and Flower Farm and School of Gardening was in Henwick, near Newbury in Berkshire. The owners and principals of the school were Miss Lily Hughes-Jones, FRHS (Fellow of the Royal Horticultural Society) and Miss Mary Peers, FRHS. They started it in 1907.

The main building was an old farmhouse in the Kennett Valley about twelve miles from Reading. The farm had four acres in crops and an orchard for fruit. It was an active business in which students learned all the practical matters needed to keep a market garden going. First, they had to learn botany and theoretical horticulture so they could pass the examinations set by the RHS. Then came subjects like fruit packing, carpentry, marketing, jam making, and even beekeeping if desired. The fashionable French method for forcing out of season vegetables was in addition to all these subjects. The students had made 400 cold frames and 1000 cloches for this work. Everything they worked on ended up going to the market.

It is not clear how many women were accepted, but it seems as though the number was small. Most of the students could live on the premises. The others found accommodation very close by. It was a nurturing environment. The principals recommended spending two years at the school in order to reap all the benefits. It cost £55 per annum with a few extras for special lessons and the use of tools. There were three terms of about thirteen weeks each. The farm remained active until the 1950s, when the land was sold and became a garden center.

School of Gardening for Women
Waterperry, near Oxford

The principal of this school, Miss Beatrix Havergal, (1901–1980) was an institution unto herself. She epitomized the movement and brought formidable powers of skill and discipline to the task. In that way she resembled the abbesses of the past. They were the CEOs and top executives of big businesses.

Waterperry was not on that scale but the determination and adherence to the highest possible standards were the same. Everyone agrees she had presence. She was actually of the next generation, having been graduated from Thatcham in 1920 with the highest honors. For a time she was head gardener at a private school for girls, Downe

House, where she designed the tennis courts. While at Downe House she met Avice Sanders. The two of them pooled their resources and opened a gardening school of their own. They moved it to Waterperry House near Oxford in 1932. Money was very tight and they needed the proceeds from the produce they grew to keep the school going.

It is possible that Agatha Christie had them in mind when she introduced the characters of the Misses Murgatroyd and Hinchliffe in *A Murder Is Announced,* two women running a market garden and small farm.[95] Miss Hinchliffe was tough and dominant while Miss Murgatroyd was soft and a little ditsy. The writer Roald Dahl is known to have had Miss Havergal in mind while delineating one of his characters. He was an enthusiastic horticulturist and a letter about this idea has been preserved.[94]

Their former student, Valerie Finnis, described the challenges of getting fragile new strawberries to market in perfect condition. Students took turns getting up in the middle of the night to check the boilers for the hothouses. There was no heat in the human dwelling but the plants were pampered.

At first all students were obliged to pay their own fees, but the authorities were so impressed by the rigor of the training they subsequently began to contribute to the support of young women who could not otherwise afford to attend. After Miss Sanders died in 1970, Miss Havergal decided to close the school and retired in 1971. Two of the graduates, Pamela Schwerdt and Sybille Kreutzburger, were hired by Vita Sackville-West to manage the gardens at Sissinghurst. They remained there for thirty years after Vita died in 1962.

PUBLIC INSTITUTIONS

LONDON COUNTY COUNCIL

The LCC supported several schools of horticulture and gardening which allowed women to attend. Lady Wolseley included them in her book *Gardening For Women*. These are the municipally supported schools she listed.

NORWOOD TECHNICAL INSTITUTE, Knight's Hill, Norwood

The courses at Norwood in south London were quite inexpensive and within the reach of a wider range of girls. Introductory and intermediate botany were offered for five shillings a course and followed by gardening classes at two shillings and sixpence. These classes were not sufficient to prepare a career but were useful additions to someone taking standard school leaving examinations. The gardening classes were given at night, allowing someone with a day job to benefit from them. It remains light in London till 10 pm in the summer.

BROWNHILL ROAD EVENING SCIENCE, Art and Commercial Centre, Catford

The fees at this school were the same as at the other one. It had a more general curriculum with biology and nature study included.

BLOOMFIELD ROAD EVENING COMMERCIAL AND SCIENCE AND ART CENTRE, Plumstead

The third of these South London schools resembled the

first one with a slightly more rigorous curriculum. These were all in modest neighborhoods, not the costly and fashionable parts of London. Politicians of that era believed in expanding educational opportunity. The premises were utilitarian and spare but the teaching was professional.

The Council employed janitors and hired gardeners to maintain these properties.

KILMORIE EVENING COMMERCIAL AND ART CENTRE, Forest Hill

The instruction at this school was planned around the syllabus of the Royal Horticultural society.

ROYAL BOTANIC SOCIETY OF LONDON, Practical Gardening School for Ladies

The Royal Botanic Society was created in 1839 by James Sowerby under a royal charter to the Duke of Norfolk. As a learned society it survived until 1932, when it was unable to renew its lease in Regent's Park. The land became Queen Mary's Rose Garden and is still open to the public, free of charge.

This school was founded in the early twentieth century and was held at the society's premises. It was officially recognized by the Technical Education Board of the London County Council. The program was for three years and consisted of extensive theory and practice, including bookkeeping for the gardener's accounts. Classes began at 9:30 am in spring and summer and 10 am in winter. Because these were day classes, the fees were less than those of the other, residential schools. Lady Wolseley comments that a number of the graduates went on to very successful careers.

UNIVERSITY COLLEGE, Reading

The University College Department of Agriculture and Horticulture was formed in 1893 under the auspices of the Board of Agriculture. Day classes in horticulture were open to anyone over the age of sixteen. Women students who could not live at home were obliged to reside in local hostels sanctioned by the college. The director of the department was a Cambridge graduate, John Percival.

The college grounds consisted of forty acres with extensive gardens and orchards which were used for teaching. Students could spend up to twenty hours a week in practical work. This was bolstered by field trips to a prominent seed company nearby, Messrs Sutton and Sons, as well as visits to the Royal Botanic Gardens at Kew. Kew was only about an hour away by train.

In the theory classes, students were prepared for the Royal Horticultural Society examinations and those of other public institutions. Lady Wolseley notes that only one young woman passed the RHS Examinations in 1904, but in 1906 three did so, and in 1907 there were six. This was less than ten percent of the total entrants.

SCOTLAND

THE EDINBURGH SCHOOL OF GARDENING FOR WOMEN, Corstophine, Edinburgh

Two graduates of the Swanley horticultural college, Miss Barker and Miss Morison, who had both gone on to take additional certificates from the Royal Botanic Garden at Edinburgh, opened their own school just outside Edinburgh at Corstophine, The Edinburgh School of Gardening for Women. They offered a broad curriculum ranging from the complete requirements for a market garden to the management of fine residential properties.

Students attended classes at the Edinburgh and East of Scotland College of Agriculture to learn the theoretical basis of the practical work they did. This thorough training meant that students had to stay at the school for two years.

Resident students lived with the principals, paying fees of £70 per annum. The school required two references from the candidates before allowing them to live there. Day students could have two daily meals at the school included in their fees of £40 per annum. The village was only few miles from the city and had good public transport.

Lady Wolseley described some of the program month-by-month, though admitting that the breakdown by month was somewhat arbitrary. March was the busiest month in the year with preparation of the seedbeds, sowing of almost every vegetable they grew as well as sowing hardy annuals in the open air and half-hardy ones in frames. Rooted chrysanthemum cuttings had to be potted out. One gets tired just thinking about it.

IRELAND

THE ROYAL BOTANIC GARDENS AT GLASNEVIN, Dublin

The Royal Botanic Gardens at Glasnevin in Dublin slowly accepted women in its classes. At first only two were accepted in 1898. By 1907, a total of eighteen women had been graduated. All found excellent positions. They worked under the personal supervision of the director himself, F. W. Moore. All lectures were free.

CONTINENT OF EUROPE

BELGIUM

In 1907 there was only one school of horticulture for women, taught by Mlle. Rossignol to a few young women at her own house in Brussels. This instruction seems to have been purely practical on a very small scale. Along with this, two government schools of horticulture accepted up to six young women and two more took three.

DENMARK

In Denmark there were no specific horticultural schools for women by 1907, but they were allowed to join the classes at public college under the same conditions as men. The curriculum at the Royal Veterinary and Agricultural College in Copenhagen lasted two years but was solely theoretical. Once they obtained their diploma, students needed to find a place to do their practicum.

Another school was Vilvorde at Charlottenlund near Copenhagen. This was for postgraduates only. It was residential and offered both theoretical and practical courses. A third school was at the Royal Gardens at Rosenborg Castle in Copenhagen. Women were not welcome and only a very few were ever accepted.

The Swedish landscape architect Ester Claesson, 1884–1931, began her career in Sweden after taking an examination in Denmark.

GERMANY

Germany had a well-established horticultural industry by 1907, particularly in Thuringia and Saxony. Great seed companies such as Ernst Benary, N.L. Christiansen, and Haage and Schmidt had been established many years before.[142] The Dippes in Quedlinburg went back for more than a century. Women are never mentioned in any of the stories told about these companies, only men. There were several excellent technical schools which provided well trained and qualified employees for these firms. As far as is known they did not accept women.

This was an era in which Germany recognized the same problem of middle class women being unable to marry for lack of a dowry, the "surplus women" of Lady Warwick. German women were, if possible, even more suffocated than those in Great Britain.[96] Helene Lange (1848–1930) was a tireless crusader for women being allowed to join in higher education and learn to support themselves. Her "Yellow Pamphlet" was a manifesto and call to arms. Lange began as a teacher of language and literature but spent her life in organizing and working for women's education. In 1887 She joined a group of women who presented a petition to the Prussian government to allow women more educational opportunities.

The petition was rejected. In the so-called *Gelben Broschüre* (Yellow Pamphlet), a companion magazine to this petition, Lange summarizes their stance on women's education 'Your goal is the teaching of girls through women, who can better empathize with the essence of girls in their view. To date, most teaching arrangements are held by men.'

Unlike women leaders in Britain she did not think so

much in practical terms but more in academic ones. Hence the idea of women becoming head gardeners or landscape architects was not developed to the same extent.

Germany had four known schools of gardening for women at that stage. They were scattered geographically but none was in Thuringia or Saxony and the one in Berlin operated in isolation from the floral industry.

DR. ELVIRA CASTNERS'S SCHOOL OF POMOLOGY AND HORTICULTURE AT MARIANFELDE, Berlin

The first substantial school intended solely for women came as a result of a very gifted female German dentist who was studying in Baltimore, Dr. Elvira Castner (1844–1923). She was so bright as a little girl that her surprisingly progressive parents sent her to a boys school to learn all the same academic subjects as the boys.

Dr. Castner was shocked to see huge crates of California apples being shipped to Germany from the port. She knew that there were great fertile plains and other suitable places in her country in which to grow all the fruit that was necessary.

Dr. Castner returned to Germany and opened her practice in Berlin in 1876, but she continued to think about growing fruit. She studied horticulture and pomology and travelled to various farms and orchards to learn what she could. In 1889, she bought land in Berlin on which to build a large house to live in and practice dentistry. Her mother and sisters planted and managed the property as a market garden. They were assisted by the porter's wife.

The wife of a local councilman had actually created the first school of horticulture for women in Charlottenburg and Dr. Castner was very intrigued with it. She was an officer of a social organization benefitting women in Germany and she eventually persuaded them to support her idea for such a school. They were very reluctant, but the school finally began in October 1894 with seven students.

The school grew rapidly and was very successful in spite of the hostility of the male gardening world. Dr. Castner offered a wide ranging and serious curriculum for the students. The school was able to accommodate up to seventy young women per year. She herself was very closely connected to the school until 1922 when it closed. The land was sold to the German railroads but the Second World War obliterated every scrap of the buildings.

Several more schools were opened but none of them were in Thuringia or Saxony near the nexus of German floriculture.

POMOLOGICAL AND HORTICULTURAL SCHOOL FOR WOMEN AT WOLFENBUTTEL

This school was run by Martha Breymann. Fraulein Breymann had nine acres with which to teach and offered either a one-year or two-year course. Both the theoretical and practical work resembled other such institutions very closely. One charming stipulation was that students were obliged to take their own feather beds and linen with them. Blankets were not allowed.

THE MARIENBURG SCHOOL FOR LADY GARDENERS, Leutesdorf

Marienburg lies near the Rhine at Leutesdorf. The

school was part of a large property, the Neuwied estate, which had both agricultural and horticultural opportunities. Frauleins Marie C. Vorwerk and Elsbeth von Zibzewik were the owners and principals. The two buildings were able to accommodate twenty students. The program lasted two years and again was very similar to all the other schools noted above. It emphasized practical skills.

Students who were not aiming at a very responsible position were allowed to take one year only. One unusual feature was that it was possible to spend a short time on site to see if the program was suitable for the young woman in question. Such students lived out.

SCHLESWIG HOLSTEIN SCHOOL OF HORTICULTURE FOR LADIES, Holtenau

Fraulein Marta Rack began her school in 1901, according to Lady Wolseley. The property was ideal, not far from the Kiel Canal. At first Fraulein Rack took in five students but then increased that number to seventeen. She and her staff taught them all they needed to know about horticulture and pomology in her orchards, large hothouses, and forcing frames. As with so many other of the schools, students needed to spend two years to reach the standard required for a high position. Less ambitious students could take the one-year course.

AUGUSTE-FORSTER INSTITUTION, OBERZWEHREN, Kassel

This school was created by the Kassel Society for the Education of Women. Young women could learn poultry keeping, horticulture, and pig rearing together with the appropriate theoretical subjects. Each course had to be taken separately. The length of study depended on how many courses the student decided to take. The Kassel Chamber of Agriculture permitted the school to use its system of instruction, set up by the Oberzwehren Pomological Institute.

UNITED STATES

The nineteenth century federal land grant system created agricultural colleges under the Morrill Act of 1862. These colleges were opened in at least nineteen states and they did not discriminate against women. Women took the same classes as the men and in view of the Civil War at the time also participated in ROTC drills on campus. Frugal state legislatures were quite pleased with this situation, as it saved them the expense of opening special institutions just for women. As a rule, these colleges served the poorer classes of people in a state, but some of them grew into major universities. Part of the foundation of the University of California at Berkeley was its College of Agriculture. This college attracted a great academic superstar of the epoch, Eugene Hilgard, and led in all soil and food-related research.

At first, women studied mathematics, soil science, and husbandry but as the century progressed and the Western states became more conventional, they were turned away from this curriculum. They were encouraged to enroll in domestic science and home economics classes instead, switched to sewing and cooking and other "womanly" courses. In other words, there was regression in educational standards and thus opportunities.

One such land grant college was the New York State College of Agriculture at Ithaca, New York. It had an extensive program with highly qualified faculty providing an excellent grounding in all the basic sciences needed. This college eventually merged to become part of Cornell University.

Theoretically equal access to these colleges meant that there was less need for private horticultural schools and colleges solely for women but a few did emerge. The Missouri Botanical Garden was a private organization but large enough to be part of the public sphere. The garden offered scholarships for men to learn horticulture but women had to pay their own way.

PRIVATE SCHOOLS OF HORTICULTURE FOR WOMEN

LOWTHORPE SCHOOL OF LANDSCAPE GARDENING AND HORTICULTURE FOR WOMEN
Groton, Massachusetts

Judith Low, Mrs. Edward Gilchrist Low, founded her school, Lowthorpe School of Landscape Gardening and Horticulture for Women, in 1901 in the same small town in which the Reverend Endicott Peabody ran his landmark preparatory school for boys, Groton. The town is surrounded by many orchards and is in prime agricultural territory.

The Lows owned seventeen acres and the extensive ornamental gardens were largely the work of the young women who attended the school. Mrs. Low encouraged a very formal style of garden design in the Elizabethan and Italian Renaissance manner.

She incorporated the school in 1909 and invited several notable academic leaders to sit on her board, such as the president of Harvard, Charles Eliot, and the director of the Arnold Arboretum, Dr. Charles Sprague Sargent. Beatrix Jones, later Beatrix Farrand, had apprenticed herself to Dr. Sargent directly when she decided she wanted to be a landscape architect. There was no suitable school for women yet and her family connections enabled her to approach Dr. Sargent with confidence.

In 1945 the school merged with the Rhode Island School of Design and the Groton campus became a convent and day school. Judith Eleanor Motley Low was descended from Benjamin Bussey, one of the founders of the Arnold Arboretum. At first the program was for two years, but it expanded to three in 1915. There was a considerable emphasis on trees and forestry with the assistance of the Arnold Arboretum. The Olmsted brothers taught landscape architecture. The distinguished German refugee artist and designer Josef Albers also taught at the school after fleeing from Germany in the early 1930s.

PENNSYLVANIA SCHOOL OF HORTICULTURE FOR WOMEN
Ambler, Pennsylvania

This was the second school for women to open in the United States. Jane Bowne Haines (1869–1937) was a Quaker who had grown up on a farm with nut orchards and a tree nursery. She rapidly absorbed everything she could about horticulture after attending Bryn Mawr College and later the New York State Library School. In addition, she spent time in England, visiting the women's gardening schools. Swanley and Studley impressed her the most. She bought land near Ambler, Pennsylvania and obtained a charter from the commonwealth of Pennsylvania in 1910. Classes started in1911.

At first there was only a small number of students, but the school slowly expanded over the next few years. All the senior positions were held by women but a few male teachers were invited for specific subjects. Miss Haines considered the goal to be a "Trained mind and a trained hand." In its day, the school was considered to be quite radical. The curriculum was the by now standard one we have seen in the other schools, but it was very broadly based and included such things as bookkeeping for those who wanted to run their own business.

In keeping with the dynamic and open-minded attitudes at the school, some of the graduates in turn did unusual things. One started the Garden Clubs of America. These graduates were instrumental in setting up Women's Land Army. Lady Wolseley must have come across Miss Haines in 1907. She asked her for an outline of her project for a school of gardening and published it in her book before the school became a reality. The school remained an independent entity until the 1950s. It eventually merged with Temple University and became Temple Ambler in 1958.

OTHER COUNTRIES

Lady Wolseley very commendably wanted to be comprehensive and so mentioned Argentina, Canada and Australia in her recital.

ARGENTINA

There were no schools specifically for women but they were allowed to sign up for the same courses as men at the universities. By 1907, only one woman had managed to reach the highest level in this system.

CANADA

Nature study was the best the Canadians could do for women at that time. Gardening was not yet considered to be a practicable profession for women. Lady Wolseley quoted from her correspondent Miss E. Ritchie of Halifax, Nova Scotia about this. Married women in remote areas were obliged to do almost all the housework and other tasks in the home because of the "servant problem." They had neither the time nor energy for heavy outdoor work.

Miss Ritchie was careful to say that she did not know about the rest of Canada, only some of it. As in other countries, public colleges permitted women to enroll in agriculture or horticulture classes if they chose.

The only outlet for women gardeners was in school gardens. One of the best such gardens was at the Macdonald School in St Anne's Bellevue, Quebec. This movement was part of general effort to improve Canadian schools for all children. Educators had been impressed by a paper at the Massachusetts Horticultural Society on creating gardens at schools. This seminal idea keeps getting re-discovered in every generation. It has been emphasized for the last ten to fifteen years in California's Bay area.

AUSTRALIA

SCHOOL OF HORTICULTURE
Richmond Park, Melbourne

In 1899 women were admitted to the School of Horticulture at Richmond Park in Melbourne. Women paid special attention to the layout and care of small residential gardens as well as the growing of vegetables and herbs. They also liked to work with table grapes and lemons. At first tuition was free, but in 1903 a fee of £5 per annum was imposed. No schools for women were established in New South Wales or Tasmania at that time.

The Australian historian Katie Holmes at LaTrobe University is studying the ways in which women were active in horticulture even without this formal component. She quoted one very condescending man, Robert Riley, saying it was better for women to be busy in a garden rather than out in the streets agitating for the vote.[109] She is writing a book about the history of women and gardening in Australia.

MARKET GARDENING

Lady Wolseley considered this to be a separate subset of women's schools, even though quite a few of the ones she described clearly offered the necessary preparation to handle it. The women emerging from Studley or Swanley were well equipped for such work. Waterperry School in the next generation could only survive because the students sold their produce at local markets.

Lady Wolseley's useful book ends with helpful advice about how to lay out new flower beds in virgin turf and other technical details. It was worth everything a hopeful young woman had to pay for it, a road map to a better future.

GARDEN CLUBS

Though not formal gardening schools, gardening clubs have also offered women the opportunity for both education and community involvement. In the United States, numerous institutions arose for the domestic amateur through the formation of garden clubs and societies. While suffragists fought for the vote and women physicians and academicians made slow gains in the professions, vast numbers of women still considered their major tasks to lie in the domestic sphere. These latter began to use their intellectual and administrative capabilities and their new college educations to organize clubs and societies to further social and civic improvements both in the United States and in England.

In the 1880s and 1890s, the Woman's Club Movement was born and swelled in ever- growing numbers, particularly throughout the United States. Some local Garden Clubs were founded at the turn of the twentieth century, such as the Floricultural Club of Covington, Georgia in 1895; the Morris Floral Club of Morris, Minnesota c. 1896 and the Wild Flower Club of Concord, New Hampshire in 1896. In 1913, the Garden Clubs of America was established as a central and federated organization. Mrs. Willis Martin, the president of one of the most active local Garden Clubs at the time, the Garden Club of Philadelphia, invited a dozen others to "share in the privilege of creating a National Garden Club." Today, the Garden Clubs of America has a selected membership of about 18,000. The Woman's National Farm and Garden Association, which was founded by Louisa Yeomans King in 1914 and was modelled after a similar organization in England, by the late 20th century had 10,000 members in branches operating in most states. Garden Clubs Inc., now National Garden Clubs, remains very active in state federations and local Clubs and focuses on education. The womanpower behind these associations presents a formidable strength.

Most garden clubs subscribe to the aims laid down by the Garden Clubs of America in 1913: "To stimulate the knowledge and a love of gardening among amateurs, to share the advantages of association through conference and correspondence in this country and abroad; to aid in the protection of native plants and birds; to encourage civic planting."

"Share advantages of association and encourage civic planting." These two factors seem to be the very opposite of the basic characteristics of the woman gardener, namely: solitude and creative individualism in her own plot, be this cottage garden, outlying homestead or suburban villa. Bell made this distinction, but there is no real tension between the two goals. A woman who is able to find relaxation and calm by gardening can join with others to do the same thing as a group.

Louisa Yeomans King, the first vice president of the Garden Clubs of America, founder of the Woman's

National Farm and Garden Association and author of ten popular books on gardening, straddled these two aspects of women and gardening with great sensitivity. She understood that women's need for solitude, which was satisfied in the peace and nurturing of the garden, must be balanced by discussion and companionable work. The kind of companionship that men could find in their work was no longer a part of many women's lives since the Industrial Revolution had eliminated many of the tasks previously allotted to women.

Throughout the twentieth century, since the early garden clubs for amateurs were founded, their members have concerned themselves largely with civic projects and conservation. Good local examples include the tree-planting projects in Pacific Heights in the early days of the San Francisco Garden Club (founded in 1926) in the late 1920s. There is a very charming story about the work of a garden club in Marin County in California at about the same time. This club had decided to plant an avenue of young trees to improve their town. When saplings are planted, they are tied firmly to stout supports so that they can grow up straight and tall. A few days after the saplings were planted, the club found them untied and blowing freely in the wind. This was attributed to vandalism and the trees were fixed, but lo and behold it happened again a few days later. This time they kept watch and found that the culprit was a gentle elderly woman who felt sorry for the trees and did not like to see them so tightly constrained.

Many years later, in a unique project, a native plant garden was created behind the Woodside Public Library in California. It was opened in 1970. This garden is planted, cultivated, and scientifically labelled by the members of the

Woodside-Atherton Garden Club. Library patrons can wander or read peacefully in this rare and delightful haven amid a glorious combination of books and flowers.

Another most impressive project is the restoration of old colonial gardens by the Garden Club of Virginia in the late 1920s and early 1930s. The money to restore Williamsburg to its former glory came from the Rockefeller Foundation. The gardens were part of that project. Many of the box hedges originally planted in the late seventeenth and early eighteenth century by descendants of British colonials had survived and were over thirty feet tall.

6

WOMEN IN LANDSCAPE ARCHITECTURE

Women began to design gardens and larger estates professionally late in the nineteenth century. The idea of well brought up young women working for hire in what was always regarded as a man's field was very jarring and took time to be accepted. There was the importance of learning something about engineering, surveying and the quality of soils. Equally important was the ability of such a woman to make sure the men gardeners under her respected her and did what she asked. They often met with insolence and hostility. A few overcame this by establishing a "reign of terror" like Ellen Willmott. (see below) A designer of gardens also has to have an almost encyclopedic knowledge of which plants will grow well under which conditions to say nothing of the question of aesthetics.

Apart from institutions like the Royal Horticultural Society or the Royal Botanic Garden at Kew there were few places in which to learn all these essentials in an orderly manner. Gardening itself had become a profession and systematized early in the nineteenth century. Joseph Paxton was probably the first major figure to come from a professional program. His designs all sprang from his own imagination based on a solid foundation.

The question whether women would design gardens differently from men is probably unanswerable. A designer must take into account not only topography and climate but most particularly the client's tastes, resources and preferences. Today there are excellent programs at numerous universities and colleges. More women than men are graduated from them. No one looking at a landscape can tell if it were designed by a man or a woman.

In the overall scheme of women's escaping the Victorian shackles landscape architects were a minute segment. Only a very few people with means can afford to employ a landscape architect but symbolically they were important.

In England, the *doyenne* was Gertrude Jekyll, 1843–1932, but she was gradually joined by a number of other serious contenders in many countries. In the United States Beatrix Farrand, née Jones, 1872–1959, occupies much the same role as Miss Jekyll. Both were esteemed not just because they were pioneers but because they did exemplary work.

Women landscape designers emerged in Germany and Austria very early. They suffered the same negative responses from their peers and had to fight discrimination time after time. The advent of Hitler meant that quite a few had to flee and at least one of them moved to California, Helene Wolf. In 1934 she left Vienna and became a teacher at the California School of Gardening for Women in Hayward.

Some women only designed one garden for their personal use, others hired themselves out to anyone needing their services. Here is a brief list of some of the better-known women landscape designers and architects. It is in no way exhaustive.

WOMEN AND THEIR PRIVATE GARDENS

VICTORIA ("VITA") SACKVILLE-WEST (1892–1962)

Sackville-West and her husband, Harold Nicolson, reclaimed the property of Sissinghurst Castle in Kent, turning it into a remarkable place which is still revered. Sackville-West credited Gertrude Jekyll with opening her eyes to the importance of colour harmony in the garden. Maybe her greatest creation was the "white garden," imitated around the world. Sackville-West was a force of nature, immensely handsome and gifted in many spheres. The diminutive first name was used to distinguish her from her mother, also Victoria. One might say Vita has almost become a legend. She was born at Knole in Kent. The house was the largest one in England and the whitest of white elephants with 365 rooms and countless fine furnishings and paintings.

Sackville-West's gardening fame was matched only by her untrammeled personal life. She had an open marriage with her husband Harold Nicolson and delighted in having freewheeling love affairs with women. Virginia Woolf's novel *Orlando* encapsulates this aspect of her life.[154] Sackville West was also a distinguished writer both of poetry and prose. This complicated set of people is well limned in "Broderie Anglaise," a *roman à clef* by Violet Trefusis, another of Vita's lovers. Trefusis' mother, Alice Keppel, was Edward

VII's mistress. Is it any wonder the public sat back with its collective mouth open, hungry for more gossip? The newspapers all thrived.

Knole had been the seat of the Sackville-Wests for centuries but as a woman she could not inherit the property when her father died. It passed to a distant male cousin. The whole business left her feeling very ill used but she did not dwell on it. For years she wrote a gardening column for the *London Observer.* These columns were collected together into several useful books. When she and Harold decided to create a garden at Sissinghurst Castle in Tunbridge Wells, Kent, that too took on a legendary quality. They bought this seemingly unpromising property in 1930 and did all the very hard work themselves. The Nicolsons were somewhat impecunious at that stage of their lives.

It is now ninety years later and thousands of visitors still flock to its gardens every year. As many as can try to copy her designs back home wherever they live. Even people who know very little about her or even about gardening at all, like the "white garden" she popularized. Its coloring seems somehow inevitable and yet it is a complete artefact.

Sackville-West acknowledged receiving a lot of her ideas from Gertrude Jekyll's books. Before Sissinghurst she and her husband had made a garden at Long Barn in Sevenoaks, Kent. Between 1915 and 1921, the Nicolsons lived in that very old house, partially dating from medieval times, and remodeled the garden. This was useful preparation for what was to come, a rehearsal as it were. Modern gardeners can still find inspiration in Long Barns' garden, though it is not open to the public very often.

· · ·

KATHERINE SWIFT (STILL ACTIVE)

Mrs. Swift worked as a librarian at Trinity College in Dublin. Her husband was an antiquarian bookseller in Oxford. Marriage at long distance began to pall, so Ken Swift scouted around for a rural property where they could live together and still let him work in Oxford. In 1988 they leased the Dower House in Morville, Shropshire, from the National Trust with the view of creating gardens of historic resonance. Her final design was, as it were, a set of "rooms," each representing an epoch in garden history. She started with the Elizabethan style. She had learned all this from the books in the college collections.

We know this story because she wrote an exquisite book about her work over the next fifteen years, *The Morville Hours,* mimicking the medieval books of hours for church observance as a framework.[140] She had a complicated childhood between her very left-wing father and a mother who hankered after spiritual experience. During the early part of her life, her mother became a Roman Catholic and brought Katherine up in that faith. Although they moved frequently for her father's work, the one constant was that he was a committed gardener. No matter where they were, he made a garden using cuttings carefully brought from the previous residence. His example embedded itself in her psyche, leading her to become an almost fanatical gardener herself.

Apart from very occasional help from a local farm laborer, Mrs. Swift did all the work by herself. Her husband knew enough to stay out of her way. The land around the house comprised old agricultural fields previously used to grow crops. Turning the primeval land into a garden required extensive preparation. She often woke up at night and wandered about in the moonlight, seeing where she wanted to place a bed or a hedge. Part of the numinous quality of her book is that she explores the nature of the earth around her, imagining what had happened to it from eons before mankind settled on it and cultivated it.

Mrs. Swift linked the pattern of her work with the book of hours and its required duties each season as a poetical conceit. When she submitted the plans for her garden, she did not use any visual aids but described the entire process solely verbally. The leasing committee of the National Trust was clearly a bit reserved about her proposals, as she had never done this before. Eventually they agreed to let her go ahead but insisted that she do it in stages rather than try to get everything done at once. That way they could monitor her progress and be sure she was not wasting their time. Although the Swifts had to move away once their lease was up in 2008, the gardens remain a National Trust treasure, with the book as its guide.

ELLEN WILLMOTT (1858–1934)

Ellen Willmott was awarded the Victoria Medal of Honour by the Royal Horticultural Society in 1897, the year the award was created to commemorate the queen's diamond jubilee. Miss Willmott and Gertrude Jekyll were the first women to be given this honor. Another woman, Eleanor Ormerod, received it in 1901 and then thirty years passed before any more women were considered. (Eleanor Ormerod was a self-taught entomologist whose lifelong work on agricultural and horticultural pests led to her being known as the "protectress of agriculture." The medal was to recognize this contribution.) The grand total of women awarded this medal reached about forty. Valerie Finnis, mentioned on page 105, was one of them.

The award of the medal to Ellen Willmott encapsulates the accomplishments of a woman who was quite unique. Today, she is remembered chiefly for the eponymous ornamental thistle, *Eryngium giganteum* 'Miss Willmott's Ghost,' and the stories of her lavish, completely reckless spending on gardens which left her almost destitute in her old age.

All this is true but does not do justice to her broad knowledge of horticulture, her solid achievements, and her quest for perfection in all her pursuits. Even if all she had done was to write the book *The Genus Rosa* that would have been enough.[151] The rose fanciers claimed her for their own. She was given the Dean Hole award of the National Rose Society, a society which had been founded by the dean, the Very Reverend Samuel Reynolds Hole. Her book was issued in two volumes between 1910 and 1914. It was profusely illustrated with watercolor pictures of her roses by Alfred Parsons. She later commissioned Parsons to paint many more of her plants.

Miss Willmott's mother was a devoted gardener and she and her sister Rose grew up watching their mother creating and maintaining gardens. Mrs. Willmott had learned from her own mother before her. She was an early adherent of William Robinson and Gertrude Jekyll in disliking carpet bedding. The distaff Willmott style of gardening was more naturalistic.

Frederick Willmott, her father, had made enough money for them to move from living above the family chemist's shop in London to buying an estate in Essex, Warley Place. The family was Roman Catholic, slightly unusual for

Victorian English society. The Willmott girls were educated at convents and were always quite pious.

When Ellen was twenty-one, she took her first step as a serious gardener by causing a rock garden to be built on the estate. Her father did not pay much attention while she hired the firm of Backhouse, famous Yorkshire nurserymen, to do it. All he asked her to do was to site the place far from his study to avoid the noise!

In any event, Ellen was independently rich because of annual birthday gifts of thousands of pounds from her wealthy godmother but had her usually careful father been paying any attention he might have been able to restrain her a bit. Although most of the planting has disappeared, the rocks still remain and one can see the outlines of this bold and beautiful section of the garden. She never looked back.

One of her initial passions was for the narcissus. When she was admitted to the Royal Horticultural Society (RHS) in 1894, they invited her as a specialist in narcissus. For years, she had been hybridizing many species of narcissus and then handing them off to nurserymen to grow under different conditions. These men finally got them distributed in the trade. She did manage to alienate E. A. Bowles, the leading amateur expert on small bulbs at the time but her work was impeccable.

As a young woman, Ellen Willmott played a very good game of tennis. She also played the violin very well at a time when women were discouraged from playing this instrument. The actions of the arms brought the bosom into great prominence and this was considered to be "unladylike." In her case, if something were good, more was better. She owned an old violin made by an Italian master but went ahead and bought another violin, a viola, and a violoncello of the same provenance.

When the future star of the viola, Lionel Tertis (1876–1975) was eleven, she allowed him to play the valuable viola. Tertis was the first modern virtuoso to play the viola as a solo instrument, compared to the violin and violoncello. He set the standard for the instrument and encouraged other musicians to follow his lead. Tertis also encouraged many composers to write music for the viola. Being allowed to play such a fine instrument was an honor for a young boy, the son of Polish Jewish immigrants.

In 1890, Miss Willmott bought property in Tresserve, a village not far from Aix-en-Provence, spending thousands of pounds on rebuilding it and refurbishing the garden. Even the nurseryman told her she could get plants more cheaply than from him. One order ran to four pages of closely written items.

The highlight of this garden was the profusion of roses. They grow very well in that part of France and she took full advantage of this. Climbing roses were dramatically displayed in trees with clouds of white, pink, and red petals everywhere.

When her father died in 1892, she inherited Warley Place as the eldest child. Even having two world-class gardens did not stop her from buying Boccanegra in Italy in 1905, eventually employing a total of 104 gardeners at her peak. None of them were women. She did not trust women gardeners, although she paid some attention to the women's horticultural schools which were springing up at the time.

The gardeners were afraid of her. She got up earlier than they did and was out there digging and weeding before they arrived at work. Her hands were deformed and discolored by the constant work. She set almost impossible standards for perfection and knew exactly where every plant was placed and if it were being properly cared for. Such a boss could be very unpredictable and thus unsettling.

Her entire existence was focused on plants and horticulture. It is said she grew 100,000 different species of plant at Warley. During her era, many plant-hunting expeditions to China and other Asian countries were organized. Miss Willmott participated financially in return for her chance to get new seed long before anyone else.

These are some of the plants which came from those expeditions: Willmott's *willmottiae* and *warleyensis* cultivars such as Veronica *prostrata* 'Warley Blue.' *Ceratostigma willmottianum*, Aethionema 'Warley Hybrid,' *Potentilla nepalensis* 'Miss Willmott,' Campanula *pusilla* 'Miss Willmott,' and *Syringa vulgaris* 'Miss Ellen Willmott' are still in commerce.

Ellen Willmott collected a comprehensive horticultural library and corresponded with all the experts of the day. As a member of several committees at the Royal Horticultural Society, she met colleagues all the time and was able to exchange views with them. Gertrude Jekyll was in awe of her.

Ellen Willmott's legacy is the more than fifty plants which were either named in her honor or which she named herself after breeding and growing them in one of her gardens. All gardeners know Miss Willmott's "ghost," *Eryngium giganteum*, sea holly. She frequently scattered handfuls of their seed when she visited other people's gardens, infuriating the gardeners. Late in her life she became quite paranoid and took to carrying a revolver with her at all times. It was a tragedy.

The buildings at Warley Place ended up being demolished and the grounds are now a public nature preserve open to all. After being abandoned and left to deteriorate, the manor in Tresserve was taken over by the village and became their town hall. Boccanegra was bought by an Italian woman who was also an excellent gardener. She was deeply conscious of the heritage in the garden. Many of the plants Ellen Willmott put in herself were still alive thirty years ago.

Looking over the trajectory of Ellen Willmott's life, she should have been a man. Had she been a man, no one would have thought she was that unusual. She had a many great gifts, she was clever and effective in everything and indulged her obsessions to the fullest. People like Lionel de Rothschild, the Duke of Devonshire, Dean Hole, Christopher Lloyd, and all those other great gardeners are praised but not considered to be extraordinary in any way, whereas Miss Willmott raised a lot of eyebrows. The fact that she lost all her money was partly to blame but it was her being so unfeminine that caught everyone's attention. Gertrude Jekyll did not arouse these responses because she remained very circumspect all her life yet she was completely iconoclastic in her way. She simply hid it more carefully.

PROFESSIONAL LANDSCAPE ARCHITECTS AND GARDEN DESIGNERS

BETH CHATTO (1923–2018)

Mrs. Chatto is famous for her book *The Dry Garden.*[92]

This is but one of a series she wrote, all quite groundbreaking in their day. Her parents were devoted gardeners and she absorbed their interest. After completing school in Colchester, Essex, she had enrolled in a teachers' training college but credited her husband, Andrew Chatto, an orchardist whom she married in 1943, with opening her eyes to the wider implications of gardening. World War II had prevented English people from learning about new ideas from Germany of setting plants into as good an imitation of their natural habitat as possible rather than simply massing them for maximum effect. The former system led to simplified, almost foolproof, gardening whereas the latter was an endless round of tasks to maintain these artificial conditions.

One of the first proponents of the more natural system was Karl Foerster in Potsdam near Berlin, who wrote on this topic as early as the 1920s. He had observed that if you put a plant into the correct environment you practically never had to go near it again once it was established. He was a great theorist but his questionable behavior during both World War II and the subsequent Communist regime in East Germany have made him controversial. Andrew Chatto knew something of this work.

The Chattos opened a nursery on a very unpromising site in Essex with dry, gravelly soil. This forced them to find plants which would grow well under such unpromising conditions. That led to her writing her now classic book. This was followed by several more, including *The Damp Garden*. Mrs Chatto frequently exhibited her work at the Chelsea Flower Show and won ten consecutive gold medals. She was so far ahead of her time that one judge scolded her for showing a "weed" in one of her displays. This was

Helleborus foetidus, "stinking hellebore," a European native plant with pale green flowers. Some radical gardeners suggest there are no weeds, only good plants in the wrong place. The fact that this particular plant flourishes against all odds in that part of your garden is telling you something. The Royal Horticultural Society awarded her its Victoria Medal and the queen invested her with the Order of the British Empire. A very impressive woman.

PENELOPE HOBHOUSE (STILL ACTIVE)

Penelope Hobhouse (née Chichester-Clark) was born in Northern Ireland in 1929. She read economics at Girton College Cambridge, one of the two colleges founded by and originally devoted to women at the university. Living and traveling through Italy she carefully noted the gardens she saw and began to write about gardens and their history. She also became a garden designer. Mrs Hobhouse's early attention to Italian gardens provided the signature structure for her designs. Not for her were wild gardens or prairie meadows. She insisted on clear sections or "rooms," defined by walls or living screens of trees or shrubs. These are the so called "bones" of a garden. Her gardens are also quite symmetrical.

Most of her working life was spent at two estates in Somerset. The first was at her husband Paul's family farm at Hadspen House. She worked very hard in the garden, keeping it in good shape but it was not until she visited Tintinhull that she understood that a garden was a place of beauty in its own right, like a work of art.

When they separated she had to move out. Her marriage to Paul Hobhouse formally ended in 1983. She had met her second husband, Professor John Malins, at a garden history meeting at Tintinhull a few years before. After marrying they became the joint custodians at Tintinhull House for the National Trust.

While she tended the garden at Hadspen she read very extensively and learned a tremendous amount from Gertrude Jekyll and William Robinson. Penelope Hobhouse has written numerous books and designed a number of well known properties, including one for the late Queen Mother in Kent. Steve Jobs commissioned her to design an English cottage garden for his estate in San Mateo County, California yet in spite of her many commissions Mrs Hobhouse considers her writing to be her most important achievement.

Mrs Hobhouse continued to grow artistically and she refined her aesthetic sense with time. At first she used a lot of bright colors but then began to turn more toward shrubs and trees with an interest in the subtler shading of the foliage. She visited Iran and was truly amazed by the beauty of Persian gardens with water being such a prominent feature and plants being more of an accompaniment. She wrote a groundbreaking book, *Gardens of Persia*.[109]

GERTRUDE JEKYLL (1843–1932)

The outstanding example of a professional landscape designer and gardener is Gertrude Jekyll. Jekyll is recognized by garden historians as an artist who revolutionized gardening design at the end of the 19th century and as a basic influence on gardeners and architects, both in England and in the United States. She visualized the importance of linking house and garden as a single unit but her most significant contribution was in making the use of color logical and harmonious.

Gertrude Jekyll had a very unusual father who gave up his military career and spent the rest of his time in amateur industrial pursuits, such as metallurgy. He insisted she learn many crafts just as seriously as a boy and to the highest standard in every case. The Jekylls all admired the work of John Ruskin and this informed much of what they did. Miss Jekyll also became a skilled needlewoman and took on many commissions for this work. She came across the well-known architect Edward Lutyens while he was still in his teens. She spotted the "divine spark" under the shy exterior and took him under her wing, obtaining commissions for him to get his career going. (Lutyens may have been the model for John Galsworthy's character, the architect Philip Bosinney in *The Forsyte Saga*.)

Known as Ned, he worked closely with her and became her friend. By the first decade of the 20th century it became fashionable to own "a Lutyens house with a Jekyll garden." While she was working very hard with all her garden designs she was also editor of William Robinson's *The Garden*, a highly influential horticultural magazine of the period. She herself wrote hundreds of brief articles for it, always detailing something she had done herself. Gertrude Jekyll was also a patron of the Glynde School for Lady Gardeners, one of the dozen or so professional schools for "Lady Gardeners" that flourished in Britain during the last Victorian decade. (See page 111)

This background gave everything she wrote a rich air of authenticity. She did not expect you to do something she had not done herself. Jekyll and Robinson both pulled the levers of change in the English garden away from the fussiness of mid-Victorian bedding out and artificiality.

In her youth, Jekyll had been an art student at the Kensington School of Art, studying with Hercules Brabazon and intended to become a painter. This in itself was very unusual for a young upper-class woman. Attending even as gentle a college as this one without a chaperone was outside the norm. She enjoyed every minute of the very demanding curriculum and kept meticulous notes. She only gave up the idea of being a full-time painter when her vision began to deteriorate and her doctor encouraged her to do something less visually taxing.

William Morris and the Pre-Raphaelites influenced her appreciation of ancient crafts and trades. This appreciation led to her study of country cottage gardens that had continued virtually unchanged for centuries around the homes of farm and village labourers.

Jekyll photographed these herself and integrated the ideas into her designs of the 1880s and 1890s. She had taught herself photography in the same meticulous way she had done with everything else. The tangle of vegetable, herb, and cascade of roses of the medieval cottage garden later inspired the informal garden of the new suburban sprawl and of ever smaller houses and gardens. She also had absorbed the science of color fluidity at Kensington based on Chevreul 's "color wheel" and planned her borders with this in mind. Chevreul recognized that we perceive a color differently when it is paired with another one. Jekyll's borders were very harmonious and pleasing to the eye.

It is perhaps no coincidence that it was a woman artist

who was equally a devoted gardener, a follower of Morris, who resurrected the essence of the medieval garden, a secluded mixture of utilitarian and pleasure garden. Jekyll's many books and articles, very popular in England, were frequently reprinted in the United States and spread by leaders of the Garden Clubs of America (including Jekyll's American friend Louisa Yeomans King).

She had a large practice and some of her gardens have been lovingly restored to their former condition. She achieved this eminence through unrelenting hard work right up to the end of her very long life. There are two charming stories about her last years. Two of her friends took their little boys to meet her when the children were about ten years old. She put her hand on their heads and blessed them. Both went on to illustrious horticultural careers.

One was Christopher Lloyd, the preeminent gardener who owned the Great Dixter estate and made it into a destination for garden pilgrims. The other was Graham Stuart Thomas, later a world-famous rosarian. He came from a working class family but she allowed him to walk around her garden and was amazed when he could name so many of her plants.

Norah Lindsay (1873–1948)

Norah Lindsay, née Bourke, was also from the Anglo Irish upper classes. Her marriage to Sir Harry Lindsay was very unsuccessful and she was thrust into the world needing to make a living. Lindsay's uncle had given them an estate at Sutton Courtenay in Oxfordshire as a wedding present. Norah turned that garden into a showplace.

Creating gardens was the one thing she could do.

Lindsay was completely self-taught, having learned by watching the gardeners at her parents' home when she was a little girl. She had an unerring eye for the appropriate plant in each location and liked to use these plants generously, often letting them spill out over a stone pathway.

Her friends began to invite her to come and re-do their gardens, thereby giving her somewhere to live cost free for long stretches of time. A noted society decorator of the period, Nancy Lancaster, promoted her generously too. Lindsay was inspired by Gertrude Jekyll but was also fond of Vita Sackville-West with her looser style of planting. It went without saying that an estate had to be well furnished with gardeners to maintain her creations.

Lawrence Johnston, a wealthy American living in England during that period, was very much at loose ends. His domineering mother decided he needed focus. She bought him Hidcote Manor in Gloucestershire and recommended Norah help him create a garden there. Norah worked closely with Johnston who had strong ideas of his own. The estate remains a place of pilgrimage for garden lovers because of its striking design as a set of garden "rooms."

Norah Lindsay also designed two gardens for Sir Philip Sassoon, one at Port Lympne in Sussex on the English Channel and the other at Trent Park near London. The latter was requisitioned by the British secret service in 1940 as an elite prison for high ranking German officers.[100] The aristocratic German generals were so flattered by the fact that they were treated with appropriate deference that it loosened their tongues when they thought they were alone. In fact the secret service had wired every single room in the building and recorded everything they said. A small army of patient transcribers worked round the clock. Most of them were German or Austrian refugees who understood German.

The garden in Sussex was built into a hillside that ran down to the coast. Lindsay made the slope into an integral part of the design rather than being a liability. Although her life appeared to be romantic and glamorous to the casual observer Norah Lindsay was a very sad figure. She was essentially penniless and actually homeless for much of the time. Her social connections and skills were such that she hid this fairly successfully most of the time. While working on a commission she had free accommodation at her employers. What little money she had was spent in keeping up her appearance. People were surprised she did her gardening in cocktail dresses and high heeled lacy sandals but these were almost her only garments. Very late in life she was dependent on the rather cool charity of her only child, her daughter Nancy. The latter also became a well-known garden designer.

Lawrence Johnston later bought another beautiful property, in Menton in the south of France and she lived there for a long time, setting up its garden. Johnston was still in England and she lived there alone. Many wealthy English people and Americans were drawn to the balmy climate and glory of the Mediterranean coast. Lindsay's exuberant abundance was a happy style in the warm Midi. It was quite contrary to the rigid discipline practiced by Baronne Beatrice de Rothschild at the Villa Ephrussi not that far away. She is said to have stationed a gardener every ten feet next to her borders, waiting to catch a leaf or blossom before it fell. No doubt this was simply scurrilous gossip but it gives an idea of what sort of garden Beatrice de Rothschild liked.

ROSEMARY VEREY (1918–2001)

Rosemary Verey, née Sandilands, read economics at University College, London but left without taking a degree to marry David Verey whose father was the rector of a village near Cirencester in Gloucestershire. They lived a typical English county life in Barnsley House, bringing up four children and joining the local hunt. She had always enjoyed growing vegetables and that was a help during the austerity period after the Second World War.

The garden at Barnsley House had been laid out by Mr Verey's grandmother but needed a lot of attention. After a hunting accident Mrs Verey was laid up for a while. Her husband bought her a book about mandrakes to help her pass the time and it caught her imagination. She began systematically to learn about horticulture and gardens, bringing all her scholarly skills to bear on the subject. The Vereys knew two important garden designers, Russell Page and Nancy Lindsay. Both helped her with concepts and Nancy also supplied plants. Now the Vereys could tackle their own garden, Rosemary knowing fully what she wanted to do and how to do it.

The result was remarkable. Almost immediately people clamored to be allowed to visit the grounds. At first she only allowed a very small number of visitors but fairly quickly it became necessary to open the garden almost every day. Charities were able to raise money by charging for the privilege of seeing Barnsley House's gardens.

Mrs Verey was inspired by classical gardens she saw in

France. Certain styles and structures became part of her palette. The famous laburnum arch was one of them. Another was restoring the use of box hedging to delineate garden sections. Making the humble kitchen garden into a work of art, the "potager" of Versailles became her best known trope. Many vegetables are naturally quite decorative such as scarlet runner beans scrambling up poles and lettuces with different colored leaves. Fava beans have big black and white flowers. Herbs had been used for centuries to make "knot gardens," complex designs like embroidery but tricked out with carefully trimmed plants.

Laying out vegetable beds in attractive patterns and surrounding them with shrubs or perennials has been absorbed into the national consciousness. Even the most casual allotment gardener will now add a few sunflowers or marigolds to his rows.

Prince Charles invited her to design his cottage garden at High Grove and remained a devoted friend until her death. She was in huge demand to prepare garden plans as well as for lecture tours and garden conferences but somehow found the time to write a number of very useful books.

INDIVIDUAL GARDENS IN NORTH AMERICA

Some women who owned private estates created astonishing gardens in very unlikely, indeed unpromising places. Two of the best known are the Butchart Gardens in Victoria, British Columbia and the Quarry Hill Botanical Garden in Glen Ellen, California. Oddly enough, both owners faced the same challenge at the outset: obsolete quarries with clifflike sides. They chose different solutions.

. . .

BUTCHART GARDENS

Robert Butchart, 1858–1943, owned Portland Cement. He bought property in Victoria on the island of Vancouver because of large deposits of limestone which was the basis of his product. He and his wife Jennie, 1866–1950, built a house on the premises, but she found staring at the ravaged hillside very distressing. Jennie Butchart was an adventurous and active woman.

To counteract this dull prospect, Jennie commissioned Isabudo Kishida of Yokohama in 1909 to help her create a Sunken Garden. He had made a wildly successful Japanese tea garden in a neighboring park. Kishida returned to Japan in 1912 but Mrs. Butchart continued to work on her plans for a sumptuous series of gardens. By 1921, they were ready to receive visitors. A boring kitchen garden and the tennis courts were both erased to make space for a rose garden and a separate garden in the Italian style, designed by Butler Sturtevant of Seattle.

Although the original plans were by a Japanese designer, the esthetic of Butchart Gardens is definitely European. More special gardens followed and today these gardens are on the Canadian list of heritage sites. The emphasis is clearly on beauty and some degree of entertainment. They are one of the most popular destinations for visitors. Presumably Mr. Butchart footed the formidable bills for all this work as atonement to his wife for dragging her to what was the back of beyond in those days. In 1939, the couple gave the property to their grandson Ian Ross as a twenty-first birthday present. He worked on it for the rest of his life, making many improvements, then dying in 1997. His great-granddaughter now owns and runs the estate.

Quarry Hill Botanical Garden

Jane Davenport Jansen, 1940–2000, bought sixty-one acres of land in Sonoma County in 1968 to build a summer home and grow grapes. About twenty years later, she decided to create a garden covering the disused quarries which were part of her property. She had spent her life in botany. Her goal was a combination of ecological preservation and beauty. She hired William McNamara to be the director and in 1987 he started travelling to Asia in the spring to identify possible plants and in the fall to collect seed. They founded a nursery in 1988 and began planting in 1990. Every plant growing at Quarry Hill comes from seed imported from the Far East, mainly China but also Taiwan, Korea, and Japan.

Quarry Hill represents a pure species garden without any of the hybrids which adorn so many other botanical gardens. Its charm comes from its authenticity. The plants have adapted very well to the California climate and terrain, even though the rain comes at different times in the year from their home territory. Roses, magnolias, lilies, and countless shrubs blossom in season. The garden is part of a consortium of similar organizations with a serious scientific purpose. Mr. McNamara, now retired, shared all this seed with Kew Gardens, Lord Howick in Northumbria, and the royal gardens at Windsor. In a few cases, the original plant has become extinct in the wild and the sole surviving germplasm is in the group's gardens.

Trees which appear to be very old because of their

height are at the most about thirty years old. Mr.
McNamara brought back seeds of the dawn redwood,
Metasequoia glyptostroboides, thought to be extinct for many
years but re-discovered in 1949 in a remote Chinese village,
growing astride the main street. They come close to the
native American redwoods in height. All of these riches
originated in Jane Jansen's vision.

CELIA THAXTER (1835–1894)

Celia Thaxter, a New England poet, 1825–1894, created
and maintained a flower garden for her family hotel on
what is now Appledore Island in the Isles of Shoals off the
coast of Maine. Mrs. Thaxter was born in New Hampshire
but moved with her family to Appledore Island. The island
had been used by seasonal fishermen for centuries, but the
permanent population was small. Her father, Thomas
Laighton, was initially employed as the lighthouse keeper
but decided to build a modern hotel and encourage New
Englanders to take their vacations there once tourists began
trickling over.

They came in droves. Most of the notables of the era
visited the island and stayed at her hotel for their summer
holidays, men like Ralph Waldo Emerson and the writer of
exquisite local stories, Sarah Orne Jewett, as well as many
other of the region's finest writers and artists: Nathaniel
Hawthorne, Childe Hassam, Harriet Beecher Stowe and
Oliver Wendell Holmes. The local people living in the
islands appear in Sarah Orne Jewett's *The Country of the
Pointed Firs.*[113] The hotel became very successful, and after
her mother died, the now Mrs. Levi Thaxter moved back to
be the hostess. Her education had been very patchy, as was

often the case with girls in that era but made more difficult by the isolation of their home. She was only able to spend one year at a school for girls in Boston. This did not affect her innate talent for writing and her earliest work was poetry about the sea. Her writing fired the public imagination and she was quite famous in her lifetime.

Celia Thaxter took her duties at the hotel very seriously. Almost as soon as she took over she planted a garden to supply its rooms with flowers but in fact there was a much richer and deeper involvement. In the last year of her life she wrote *An Island Garden*.[144] Beneath the predictably syrupy opening, the book offers really useful gardening information. Her war on the cutworm is not a pretty sight. The cutworm's appearance is loathsome and it can only be controlled by picking the critters off one at a time by hand.

Thaxter's garden is still maintained in pristine condition by the scientists and students and faculty at the Shoals Marine Laboratory and may be visited from time to time. Reaching the island in the institute's vessel sounds like a rugged experience.

None of this would have been so notable without Childe Hassam's famous paintings. Through him the gardens became widely known. All the references are to "Mrs Thaxter's garden." No one mentions her husband or anyone else having anything to do with it. She and her husband did not get along well and often spent time apart. He did not live on the island with her.

Mrs. Thaxter's garden layout and seed list are still available.[145] Perhaps the most striking thing about the seed list is the sheer number of varieties of flower she grew, at least fifty. One wonders where she bought them. The age of the heavily illustrated nursery catalogue with colored pictures was just beginning. James Vick in Rochester, New York, issued the first known catalogue with colored pictures in the early 1870s.

There were reputable seedsmen in New England and upstate New York at the time. Apart from James Vick, Ellwanger and Barry were supreme in Rochester and supplied customers all over the country. In Massachusetts James Breck of Boston was perhaps the best-known seedsman, but there were many others, such as the Farquahar family.

Beside buying her seeds at a nursery, Mrs. Thaxter may also have obtained bulbs and cuttings from generous friends. Gardeners are renowned for their desire to share good things with others.

The compilers of the seed list pointed out that the list offers a low estimate of her choices, that in fact other plants were grown which were never on it. Her principal criteria were that the flowers should be suitable for cutting, i.e. have long stems and be very brightly colored. She adored any kind of poppy and grew at least six types. Poppies are predominant in Hassam's paintings of her property. Hassam struggled to reach success, starting out as an Impressionist when that was still suspect, but ending up as sort of "Grand Old Man" of the genre, even becoming quite rich in the process.

PROFESSIONAL LANDSCAPE ARCHITECTS FOR HIRE

BEATRIX JONES FARRAND (1872–1959)

Beatrix Jones was born into the highest echelons of New York society, "The 400," a society her aunt Edith Wharton portrayed so perfectly in her novels. Beatrix must have been as focused as her aunt, following the path they wanted in spite of a lot of discouragement that ladies did not do these things. Mrs. Wharton commissioned striking gardens in France and in Lenox, Massachusetts.

Through her family connections, Beatrix managed to get Charles Sprague Sargent, director of the Arnold Arboretum in Jamaica Plain near Boston, to accept her as his apprentice. This was the only way she could learn the craft at the time. The arboretum is affiliated with Harvard University.

FLORENCE YOCH (1890–1972)

Florence Yoch is remembered as the landscape designer to the stars in Hollywood and for "Tara," the grounds she designed for the film *Gone With The Wind* but her practice was much broader than that.

She was born in Santa Ana, California and spent an active childhood in the outdoors with her five sisters. Her family owned a hotel in Laguna Beach and she was exposed to a wide circle of artistic friends. She seemed to have known from early on that she wanted to design gardens. Yoch started college at the University of California at Berkeley and then transferred to the School of Agriculture at Cornell. She completed her studies in landscape architecture at the University of Illinois at Urbana-Champaign and then set up in practice.

Yoch had her own style, meshing European formality with a truly American spirit and designed a wide range of gardens for private residences and public parks. As her practice grew, she took Lucille Council on as a partner.

7

WOMEN IN ORNAMENTAL PLANT
BREEDING

Historical shorthand may be a sign of mental laziness but does help to crystallize the spirit of an epoch. A large part of the eighteenth century became known as the "Age of Enlightenment." By contrast I submit that the nineteenth century was the "Age of Improvement." Everything except perhaps human behavior was up for radical redoing. In the "macro-sphere" roads and bridges replaced muddy tracks and fords. Railways made travel faster and more reliable once they got the kinks out. Public sanitation reduced the repeated outbreaks of deadly diseases and the new industrial cities were at last represented in Parliament. Mass production of everyday goods made them cheaper and more accessible.

In the "micro-sphere" there were large advances in chemistry, physics, geology, biology and astronomy. New and better flowers were among this group. Some florists were driven by sheer curiosity, the "what if" brigade. Introducing a brighter, longer lasting flower with resistance to the common diseases was not only a satisfying challenge in itself but could bring the developer considerable wealth at time when the general level of prosperity rose and more people could buy a house with a bit of land around it to lay out a garden.

The human race has responded to the enchantment of flowers over millennia. There is evidence of their importance in religious ritual from the pyramids at Giza. Garlands of an ancient lotus were recovered from the tomb of King Tutankhamen. Eons passed before people began to think of making any changes to what they found growing around them or at least left any record of trying to do that but it was inevitable that they would. Restless curiosity is a hallmark of being human.

There are two principal ways of changing flowers. One is by direct selection as distinct from natural selection and the other is by cross fertilization. Cross fertilization within species can occur spontaneously in nature or intentionally by human choice. Cross fertilization between species usually only take place under human control.

Selection is epitomized by farmers saving seed from the best performing plants to sow the following year. Gardeners did the same with their favorite flowers. A station master's wife in rural upstate New York saved the seed from her beloved sweet peas and planted them year after year for more than thirty five years. She had poor quality soil and not many advantages but the sweet peas were fragrant and tough. When the prominent seedsman Dexter Ferry visited the town he was very impressed by these flowers and bought the rights to them there and then. He subsequently released them as his cultivar *L.* 'Blanche Ferry' to great acclaim.

From that prudent and conservative behavior it was not

a big step to looking actively for improvement and even novelty. The use of selection started early and persisted into the modern era. Possibly its earliest known use was in China. When Western explorers found new, previously unknown, types of flower in China in the nineteenth century, the specimens they brought back with them from the few coastal cities they were allowed to visit and thought were new species had been improved almost continuously for millennia. That fact only emerged when modern plant hunters visited the interior of China and found the original species of rose or peony without the modifications of selection.[148]

If the gardener wanted to change the color of the blossoms this is one way it could be done. A row of plants with yellow flowers might include one that had lighter colored blossoms. The observant gardener saved that plant's seed separately and sowed them the following season. Technically the light blossoms were a mutation or "sport" of nature. Trying to grow all the plants to bear the lighter colored blossoms added novelty to prudence.

The introduction of a pure white marigold resulted from this process. Such a flower does not occur in nature. David Burpee, owner of Burpee Seed and a fanatic about the marigold, had offered a prize of $10, 000 in 1954 to anyone who could develop seed for a large flowered marigold with snow white petals. No sufficiently pale marigold had ever been found in the past so the money was safe but as with almost everything else Burpee did, it was a huge marketing ploy. Thousands of people bought seed to compete in this challenge.

One such person was Alice Vonk, 1908–1997, the widow of a farmer in Iowa. Her garden was the center of her life and she decided she could win the prize. It took her about twenty years but she did it. She used the simplest of all methods outlined above. She started out with light yellow marigolds and saved seed from the plants with the palest flowers every season. The next year she planted only those seeds and once again watched for paler colors. After about ten years she had some very attractive light ivory marigolds and sent them to Burpee. They were listed for sale in his catalogue. She was not alone. He gave five of these amateur breeders $100 each to encourage them but did not hand out the $10,000.

Burpee reckoned without Mrs Vonk's incredible patience. In 1975 she found exactly what she wanted, snow white marigolds with two and a half inch blossoms. She had won the prize. Mrs Vonk had no training in horticulture or genetics but was simply a member of the public. As she put it, she was just "fooling around in the garden."

This system of selection was used for animals too. When a stallion won many races and was clearly superior to the competition, horse breeders used that stallion to get as many foals as possible. Sheep breeders bred merino sheep for longer, softer wool fibers and cattlemen worked to improve the yield of their milch cows or beef cattle. All of this activity was done under the rubric of selection. Because of the importance of food all improvement in crop yield and quality was life giving. Everything these farmers did was completely empirical. The practitioners had no idea yet of the scientific principles which lay behind their results. A general recognition of those principles would not emerge before the very last year of the nineteenth century when the work of Gregor Mendel was rediscovered after a lapse of forty years.[131]

In eras when a belief in a god or gods reigned supreme, gods who controlled all life and death, making this sort of change did not raise any eyebrows. Farmers were simply working with what God had provided. They were not transgressing. The drawback of continuing with selection was that the results were not entirely predictable and it took a very long time to go from one season to the next. Mrs Vonk had to wait twenty years for her reward. Short-circuiting the process began to look attractive.

The process of cross fertilization within a species was always taking place without human intervention. Fertilization was carried out by natural forces such as the wind carrying pollen or bees doing the same thing. Certain plants depended on it for survival. Sweet corn usually pollinates itself but needs the wind to carry its pollen. Without bees there would be almost no almonds. Magnolia trees need beetles to fertilize them. Magnolias arose at a time in evolution when insects had not yet appeared.

Some of Luther Burbank's important discoveries came from this system. He grew all his experimental plants out in the open and examined the results frequently. Burbank had a very clear sense of what he wanted to accomplish and could tell at a glance whether a new specimen had potential, whether it arose by passive selection or cross pollination. Natural self and cross pollination was so pervasive that once breeders wanted to study only certain instances of cross breeding they had to take measures to protect their experimental plants. Female flowers were stripped of their petals to prevent the bees from finding them attractive. Blue and red corn had to be grown in separate fields to keep the colors pure.

It was when a human being decided to cross two species intentionally that religious hackles rose. In 1720 a London nurseryman, Thomas Fairchild, holding his breath, took pollen from a "Sweet William," *Dianthus barbatus* and placed it on the style of a carnation, *Dianthus caryophyllus*. This hybrid produced seed of an entirely new form of dianthus. When he displayed it to his colleagues they named it "Fairchild's mule." A stem with a blossom survives in the Oxford University Herbarium. Fairchild was both elated and terrified. He had defied God and usurped His prerogative of creating a new species of plant. For the rest of his life Fairchild adhered very closely to all the religious rituals at his church and left his estate to the church to sponsor an annual lecture in perpetuity, praising the creative powers of God. The last lecture was given in 1942 before the church was bombed in World War Two.

Over the following century small experiments of this type were undoubtedly made but the scientists and florists who did it hedged their bets by naming the resulting flowers as a new, previously unknown but often very dubious sounding "species." In 1751 a pupil of Linnaeus, Peter Osbeck, sent a new kind of rose to England from China via India, *Rosa chinensis* var. *spontanea*, the "China Rose." One of the first Englishmen to grow it was a Mr Parsons just outside London. People spoke of the flower as "Parson's Pink China." It was a slight little thing, quite unobtrusive but it had one characteristic that was dynamite. It bloomed more than once in the season.

No known Eurasian rose at the time was able to do that. Perhaps because the actual blossom was small and not very exciting it took a while for this feature to sink in. Some years later the nurserymen woke up.

Putting any thought of possible excommunication aside they quite openly crossed 'Parsons Pink China' with their existing stock of roses, determined to take advantage of the second flush. Rose breeding and later all flower breeding never looked back. By the 1830s it was no longer necessary to employ subterfuges. The church backed down in face of this onslaught and did not excommunicate anyone. Some of those early enthusiasts were themselves clergymen.

A few very visionary men established huge commercial nurseries specifically to create as many new hybrids as they could. Louis Van Houtte, 1810–1876, was among the first to do it. He built extensive greenhouses in Ghent, Belgium. Victor Lemoine, 1823–1911, from Eastern France, studied with him soon afterwards and opened his own nursery in Nancy in 1843. These two men introduced literally hundreds of new varieties, or cultivars as they are known technically, across the entire spectrum of florists' flowers and shrubs. No one has ever surpassed their efforts. Every time you walk into a supermarket and see seven different kinds of gladioli or five kinds of carnation that exciting choice all stems from the work of Van Houtte and Lemoine.

Intentional plant breeding was now an accepted part of agriculture and horticulture. There were two separate streams of activity. One was the private hobbyists who had an obsession with one type of flower, very often roses, and then there were the professional breeders who are now employed by large vertically integrated nurseries and seed companies, working on whatever they have to do for the firm.

A third phase is hovering in the distance. With advances in molecular biology the use of both selection and macroscopic hybridization is going to recede very slowly. However skillfully the breeder works with known phenotypes, (specific plants), based on their heredity, that is still not as specific as taking an actual gene with the properties you are seeking and inserting it directly into an experimental plant. The next time that plant sets seed the new characteristic has been embodied in it. At present this remains a costly and cumbersome method but the signs are very clear. It will be the way of the future.

Both men and women do exceptional work in the private hybridizing sphere. In some cases the large firms actually depend on these breeders for rare plants which it does not pay them to invest in very heavily but which they still need for some purposes. Most amateurs fund their own experiments for the pleasure of it. The universities started setting up research centers such as the one run by Sir Rowland Biffen of Gonville and Caius College at Cambridge to pursue improved versions of wheat. The independent John Innes Center in Hertfordshire, England and others like it were established to exploit the new knowledge.

The mood was one of constructive ferment. True to form the participants were almost all completely men. They peopled the universities, the large commercial nurseries and academic research. Women were not in those fields and no one really thought about the possibility that they might contribute anything to the new discoveries. In the information which follows it will be seen that many women introduced outstanding cultivars in their capacity as either amateur gardeners or owners of nurseries themselves.

They have not been employed in large numbers in the institutions whether academic or commercial. At a very rough estimate they form about ten percent of the work force. Almost none are in agricultural crop breeding. More women now develop new and better vegetables. Some of the women who are in professional plant breeding concentrate on ornamental crops, ie flowers.

Choosing to become a plant breeder requires a certain combination of skills and personal traits. We have already alluded to patience. Time is measured in years, not weeks or months. An orderly mind and retentive memory are absolutely required. Every move must be carefully documented for the results to be worth anything. There is a cautionary tale about one enthusiastic amateur breeder of rhododendron in Massachusetts who was very generous with his floral offspring. Forty years later experts are still scratching their heads as to which cultivars he distributed. Usually a pedant is one who is despised but in plant breeding a touch of pedantry can be very helpful.

The academic and technical requirements include a good working knowledge of biology and genetics. Physical dexterity is also important. Then there are imagination and flair. Many flower breeders start with an idea of what their new flower should look like, a vision. Then they must have the extra intuitive sense to identify it when they see it even if in an unlikely setting.

There is the story of Montague Allwood whose family had bred dianthus for years. Every year the staff planted out dozens of new varieties. The owners and experienced team leaders culled them as they blossomed. In that particular year one of the owners, Montague Allwood, had thrown out a pink dianthus which did not meet his criteria. His foreman thought otherwise and secretly rescued it from the scrap heap. The foreman put it in a quiet corner of the nursery and began propagating it. When Monty saw the result he was pleasantly surprised and agreed it should be kept. He named it for his wife, Doris. *D.* x *Allwoodii* 'Doris' turned out to be a perennial best seller for years. No one is infallible.

The final qualification is a completely ruthless honesty. No sentimental consideration should stop the breeder from discarding something which is not exactly what he or she wants no matter how much effort went into its creation. An also ran is not good enough.

No doubt someone will raise the question of whether there is any difference between the approach of women to breeding new flowers compared to that of men. The short answer is no. The gifts of imagination and vision are not limited by gender. Both men and women are capable of knowing the mechanics and science of their calling sufficiently well to plan a path toward a new cultivar and adhere to it. Mythical gifts of color recognition and refinement are said to favor women but that has no foundation in fact. Men are as perfectly well able to develop flowers with great subtleties of coloring as women and both sexes come up with exquisitely fanciful shapes of petals and sepals.

In the account which follows it would be invidious to give greater weight to any one flower over another but the reality is that the rose occupies a very special place in the public imagination. Roses represent special occasions and moments of emotional intensity to say nothing of being the national flower of the United States. It has occupied this place for many centuries.

The Romans were preoccupied with them and grew them in enormous quantities. The Emperor Heliogabalus used them to murder some unwanted guests by suffocating them in a deluge of rose petals. In fifteenth century England red and white roses were the badges of two aristocratic warring factions. For these reasons I shall mention rose breeders before any others. Even so this can only be a partial listing.

ROSE BREEDERS

CECILIA LUCY DAPHNE PANTON, always known as "Dee," 1921–1988, grew up in Western Australia but married an American sailor by the name of Bennett and moved to Chula Vista near San Diego, California, soon after World War Two. The first plant she bought for their otherwise bleak back yard was a rose bush. Mrs Bennett joined garden clubs and gradually became quite expert with plants and flowers. One man influenced her more than any other, Ralph Moore in Visalia, the leader in miniature rose development. He explained how to develop these tiny plants and set her up with many gifts. What had been a charming hobby became a small but flourishing business, the "Tiny Petals Nursery." The American Rose Society gave her its award of excellence on two occasions and was considering another award when she died. Her mother survived her and Dee Bennett was buried in Australia.

MARIE "LA VEUVE" DUCHER

Marie, "La Veuve," Ducher's husband was a successful nurseryman in Lyons. After he died she carried on the business, introducing important new roses. Her daughter Marie married Joseph Pernet, in 1881. He had studied hybridizing with Alegatière, a leading developer of dianthus and from there moved on to Madame Ducher to improve his knowledge of roses. He later took over the business. In order to placate his new family Joseph Pernet had attached the name of Ducher to his own. His mother in law had introduced the vigorous climbing polyantha, *R.* 'Mlle. Cécile Brunner,' which is still widely grown.

Very little biographical information is available on La Veuve Ducher but the names of her male descendants are carefully recorded. The family still runs a rose nursery, now in its sixth generation. Unlike La Veuve Clicquot of champagne fame, Madame Ducher, who was equally as capable, has been consigned to the shadows.

JIANG EN-TIAN

Jiang En-tian, 1908–1975, was known affectionately as the "Rose Lady" during her lifetime. She was born in Taicang, Jiangsu Province. Taicang lies near the Yangtse River and was an important shipbuilding city and port in the 15th century. Admiral Zheng set off on his enormous voyages from this city in 1421 in the name of the emperor Zhu Di.

As a young woman Jiang studied Western literature at Qinghua University (now Tsinghua University) in Beijing but later in her life worked exclusively on roses. From the 1950s, Jiang En-tian established many of the important bases of modern rose classification in China, identifying early cultivars as well as breeding new ones.

She began her career as the unexpected heir to an elderly physician, Dr Wu Lai-xi. Dr Wu had studied in England and had imported more than 200 European rose cultivars over the years. As he grew older he started to look for someone who cared deeply about roses, who had enough space to keep all the plants in good condition and who knew English well enough to read his books about roses.

Jiang En-tian fitted these criteria. Dr Wu died in 1951. Even though her husband's work took them away from Beijing to Tianjin, she successfully moved the roses to Tianjin and pursued her career. There were about 400 roses in his collection. Within about 5 years she became expert, partly from the books and partly from her own experience.

One of her classmates at the university rose through the political ranks to become the vice mayor of Beijing. He knew about her work and in 1958 asked her to create a rose garden at the Great Hall of the People to celebrate the tenth anniversary of the New China. In a fairly short time Jiang built four rose gardens, one in Beijing and the others close by. She spent more than 7 years commuting between Tianjin and Beijing every week and accepted no pay from the Chinese government.

She must have been very adept at politics. The next thing we know is that she donated all her roses to the people of China. She bred more than 3000 cultivars and placed the best of them at the Great Hall of the People. To commemorate her work, Taicang created the Entian Rose Garden. A senior official of the China Biodiversity Conservation Foundation planted a specimen of *R.* 'Entian Lady' in the park. This official may well have been

ZuoShuang Zhang, chairman of the Chinese Rose Society and a member of the foundation's botanical committee.

Jiang En-tian also worked in the gardens around the Temple of Heaven, the fifteenth century monument in Beijing near the Forbidden City. These grounds provide a peaceful place in which the citizens of Beijing can relax and enjoy doing their exercises.

Jiang En-tian's son, Chen Di, showed his mother's roses to Hazel LeRougetel, a prominent English mid-20th century rosarian, when Mrs LeRougetel visited China in 1985. They came as a complete revelation. He remained in communication with Mrs LeRougetel for a long time but eventually moved to the United States in 1987, to continue his work as an engineer. He lives in Marin County, California.

GLADYS FISHER

Gladys Fisher (1894–1993) worked in Woburn, Massachusetts, in the mid twentieth century. She is best known for the introduction of 'Sterling Silver," an extremely pale lavender colored blossom. Her husband, Frank Gordon Fisher, was a nurseryman but she was a rose breeder in her own right. The Arnold Fisher nursery ran from 1916 to 1975. Gladys Fisher was born in Dover, New Jersey and educated at New Hampshire College.

OLIVE FITZHARDINGE

Olive McMaster, 1881–1956, was born into a wealthy Australian family and married a scion of the old Fitzhardinge family. The Fitzhardinges lived in a large mansion surrounded by at least four acres of land. She and her sister had been influenced by the Arts and Crafts movement and this guided her choice of interior and exterior designs.

Roses attracted her and she began to cultivate them and later cross breed them very seriously. Eventually she registered twelve cultivars between 1932 and 1939. The best known one is 'Warrawee.' Behind the genteel façade of a great estate she was said to operate her rose growing as a commercial business. As part of her activities she set an important precedent in Australian horticulture. The country had no system of patents for new plants. In order to protect her work she applied for patents in other countries.

MARIE LOUISE MEILLAND

Marie Louise (Louisette) Meilland, nee Paolino, 1920–1987, was the wife of Francis Meilland, the creator of the 'Peace' rose. This rose was smuggled safely out of France just as the Germans were advancing. The seedlings were entrusted to Robert Pyle, owner of Conard Pyle and a great connoisseur of roses. Francis had named it 'Madame A. Meilland' at first but after 1945 when it was released in the United States it became the 'Peace' rose. Francis died very young in 1958 but Marie Louisette took charge and ran the business until her son Alain was old enough to manage it. She was an excellent rose breeder in her own right and left a legacy of 120 new cultivars. Marie liked to name her flowers for well known people like Princess Grace of Monaco or Maria Callas. One was called 'Pink Panther.' She never wanted her own name used but her grandchildren finally got round that by naming a new rose 'Manou Meilland' (manou is a version of grandma.)

Nola Simpson

Mrs Simpson was born in 1930 in New Zealand and died in 2001. She introduced the first brown floribunda rose, 'Hot Chocolate' into commerce in 1978. This unusual rose won many awards and was followed by others in similar colors. For many years she worked as a computer scientist, teaching at Massey University. Rose breeding was her hobby and she pursued it with the same rigor she applied to her mathematics. One of her chief rivals on the rose bench was John Simmons. Eventually they declared a truce and got married.

The other roses she bred were so outstanding she became a leader in the field, elected to all the offices of the rose organizations in New Zealand and receiving a life time achievement award from the Royal National Rose Society of the United Kingdom.

Felicitas Svejda

Felicitas Svejda, 1920–2016, was born and educated in Vienna, but after WWII went first to Sweden and then in 1953 to Canada. She had been trained in genetics and was employed by the Department of Agriculture at the Central Experimental Farm in Ottawa. This was the same department where Isabella Preston had done such outstanding work. They overlapped for about ten years. It is intriguing to wonder if they met and chatted about their work. People who knew her recalled she was very distant and formal because of her Austrian upbringing.

At first she was relegated to a desk job but it soon became clear she was most unusual and she was instructed to develop a line of cold hardy, recurrently blooming roses which would flourish in Canada with its harsh winters. Dr Svejda achieved this by using an extremely tough species rose, *Rosa Rugosa,* as one of the parents. Her philosophy was simple. The seedlings were planted out in open fields and had to survive on their own without any coddling or pampering. Whichever one was left standing at the end of several winters then entered the next phase of her trials. Many years before, John Gable in Pennsylvania had used this system to breed a whole new class of modern rhododendrons.

After eight years a tough attractive rose emerged which was adopted on a very wide scale. Dr Svejda had produced the "Explorer" series. They not only do well in Canada but in many sub-Arctic northern European countries with long winters like Finland and Norway. In addition to their cold tolerance these roses also resisted many common pathogens. Svejda turned to Canadian history for names such as 'William Baffin' and 'Samuel Champlain.'

Girija Viraraghavan

Dr Viraraghavan has spent more than fifty years working with her husband S. Viraraghavan jointly breeding roses to suit the Indian climate. They live in Kodaikanal in the Western Ghats at an elevation of 2000 meters. He retired from the Indian Agricultural Service at the age of forty two to devote himself to breeding roses. Girija was an historian and not active in floriculture when they met and married. Her maternal grandfather had been president of India in the mid 1960s and she had many social duties as a result. That soon changed.

Neither Girija nor her husband has any formal training in horticulture. S. Viraraghavan became enchanted by roses at the age of eleven and essentially taught himself everything about them under the guidance of mentors. His father made sure he took the right exams and prepare for a career but nothing overcame the attraction to roses. Girija claims that everything she knows about the flowers comes from her husband.

Many species of roses found in other parts of the world are also native to India. The rose has been part of Indian culture for thousands of years and it is used for many purposes. Once India established commerce with China new roses found their way into the country. On top of that English families gradually brought their own familiar roses with them over two centuries. By the time Girija and her husband started their work they had a great variety of roses to use for crossing.

The Viraraghavan's house is shaded by a yellow hybrid *Rosa gigantea* they bred themselves many years ago. Quite a few of their roses are named for friends all over the world and there is a park in Tokyo devoted to their work.

SISTER MARY XAVIER

Sister Mary, 1910–1995, was a Presentation sister at a convent in Tasmania. She was born Mary Irene Lewis-Hickman in Devonshire but moved to Tasmania in 1930. At one time she was a vice president of the Rose Society of

Tasmania. The "Rose Sister" was a staunch exhibitor at the local rose shows in Hobart and Launceton. At the very end of her life she cut the flowers for a rose show the following day, including a new red rose which had not yet been registered. Alas, she was not well enough to attend the show and died on the following day. Sister Mary taught at St Finn Barr's College and instilled her enthusiasm into many girls. The girls held their own rose shows at school and followed all the rules set by the adult society.

Sister Gabrielle Morgan, leader of the Tasmanian Congregation of Presentation Sisters, shared these comments with me:

"On ten occasions she won the Grand Champion Award for the best rose in the Launceston Horticulturalist Society Show. Her biggest thrill came on 11 November 1989 when she won the Grand Champion Award at the Tasmanian Rose Society Show in Hobart.

Sr Xavier had one rose registered which earned her great praise and income for the Sisters: 'Iced Parfait' and also entered a second one, the 'Nano Nagle' rose (after Nano Nagle, Foundress in Ireland of the Presentation Sisters). Unfortunately, that one was not accepted for registration but the Sisters enjoyed taking cuttings and growing those roses in their gardens."

ASTERS

Elizabeth Bodger

Elizabeth Bodger, 1904–1943, (Mrs Herman Baerschtiger) was the daughter of Walter and Katharine Bodger and grand daughter of the founder of Bodger Seed in Central California, John Bodger. She was the eldest of four children and thus very much used to taking care of others and assuming a lot of responsibility. Elizabeth wanted to go to college and in spite of the usual grumbling about wasting money on a girl's education she did go and earned a bachelor's degree in Romance language at Pomona College. She then did a master's in horticulture at Cornell University's school of agriculture. Her knowledge of Spanish was an asset in dealing with the employees.

With her degree in plant science she was appointed chief horticulturist and hybridizer to the firm. There was plenty to keep her busy. It is entirely likely that she would have been taught by the eminent Liberty Hyde Bailey, 1858–1954, at Cornell, as well as possibly his daughter Ethel Zoe. Bailey transformed rural America with his innovative programs of establishing practical organizations for farmers, teaching and publications.

In the 1920s no other American seed company had a scientifically educated woman as its chief hybridizer. At that time asters were very popular and Bodgers grew them on a vast scale. The trouble was that they were prone to fungal infestation, "fusarian wilt." The company needed to find a way to protect the plant from the fungus to restore the public's confidence. Elizabeth Bodger consulted with experts on fusarian wilt at the University of Wisconsin and planted numerous aster cultivars in a field known to contain the fungus. She then watched what happened over three years. Eventually enough plants emerged which were resistant to the fungus to restore their commercial line to health. The Bodger catalogue for 1931 offered six resistant asters.

This was not her only task. She managed all the work associated with growing reliable and viable seed, watching out for faults which can creep into any mono-crop. She had a team of five employees working on these diverse tasks.

Her care and resourcefulness enhanced Bodger's already excellent reputation. The All American Trials council appointed her to its committees to select the best new floral introduction of the year. Elizabeth Bodger also wrote a syndicated column for the New York Times, focusing mainly on vegetables during World War Two. In addition she was in demand as a speaker and actively promoted the Bodger company. She developed numerous cultivars of larkspur, calendula, cosmos, nasturtiums, zinnias, dianthus and chrysanthemums. During the Depression gardening was one pastime even the poorest could afford and seed was cheap.

She believed she had made a real contribution to the family firm and asked her father for a raise after a year. He rejected her request, saying she was "merely a woman." She did not hang around after this injustice. Elizabeth Bodger left Bodgers and went to teach in a local school. It did not take long for the family to invite her to return.

In 1936 she married Herman Baertschiger, an eligible bachelor in El Monte where she lived. Once she became pregnant she resigned from Bodgers in spite of her family's entreaty she merely take maternity leave and return when she was ready. This was not to be. Elizabeth Bodger Baertschiger died of a pulmonary embolism five days after a Caesarean section for her son Robert in March 1943. The entire town closed down for her funeral.

At some time in the 1930s the All America Selection organization awarded her their gold medallion. Neither the date nor the reason for the award were recorded.

CLEMATIS

MARGARITA BESKARAVAJNAJA

Margarita Alexeevna Beskaravajnaja, 1928–2003, was born in a small town in South western Russia and attended the university at Voronezh. She must have been a very able student to be allowed to enroll at the Moscow State University for post graduate studies in botany and plant science. This was in the late 1940s when the USSR was still profoundly depleted by the Second World War. As with the case of Mikhail Orlov she must have been completely apolitical.

After university she took a job at the State Nikitsky Botanic Garden in Yalta and worked there for more than thirty years. A. N. Volosenko-Valenis joined the staff while she was there. After he died she took over his unique collection of clematis and continued his work with the assistance of Helena Donyushkina. Although Beskaravajnaja was far from the centre of things she kept close contact with the rest of the horticultural world and wrote books and articles about her work. She introduced more than two dozen cultivars. Many Western gardeners have heard of *Clematis* 'Aliosha.'

MARIA FODOROVNA SHARANOVA

Maria Fodorovna Sharonova, 1885–1987, must have been a most remarkable woman, quite apart from living to be 102 years old through a tumultuous century in which the Russia she had known became the USSR and an exceedingly dangerous place to live. After college she became a botanist and worked for many years on dahlias.

Very late in life Sharanova decided to breed short clematis plants in bright colors, suitable for Moscow balconies and window boxes. It is not clear what inspired her to do this but even in her late 90s and bedridden she was still active in this program, albeit now managed by other people.

Moscow's climate is very forbidding because it is so far north. There is not enough time for clematis to set seed every summer so Sharanova might not get seed for two or even three years. Eventually she left more than 200 cultivars of which forty were named and introduced. Although she set out to create shorter forms there were also taller, very free flowering ones among this number. The names are all in Russian. Few of them are familiar in the Western world.

DIANTHUS

LAETITIA MOUCHEBOEUF

Laetitia Moucheboeuf works in England but grew up and was educated in France. She is from a farming background and always enjoyed being in the garden, helping her mother and grandmother. She began her higher education at La Rochelle University in France and then moved to Angers University. It was well known at the time for horticulture. She followed this with further training in plant biology and genetics ending with a master's degree.

During this period she worked in various related jobs but always with a view to start breeding plants one day. Her effort was rewarded. Within six months of completing her masters she was offered the position of plant breeder at the English firm of Whetman. She thinks she was taken on because all the other work she had done gave her a very wide range of skills, not just in plant breeding.

Laetitia told me "We use the classical method where pollen of one plant is applied on the other and we collect the seeds, sowing and selecting seedlings that look interesting. Everything is tracked in minute detail of course. As our product comes from vegetative propagation, we have to test these selected plants thoroughly and from start to finish. I would say it takes up to six years to bring to the market a new variety to market. We probably raise 10 000 seedlings per year but only two or three will end in the catalogue. And every year, we have different generations to look at, depending at which stage they are."

ECHINACEAE

JIAN PING REN

Jian Ping Ren was born and educated in China. She studied horticulture and genetics and joined the government research service breeding new vegetables. Ten years later she went to the United States on an exchange program in New York where she worked with Professor Michael Dixon of the USDA Germplasm Collection at Cornell University. She obtained a doctorate and then moved to California in 2001 to work for PanAmerican Seed.

Dr Ren has introduced numerous new flower cultivars but is most interested in the *Echinaceae* or coneflowers. Many are native to the United States and lend themselves to garden use. She broadened the range of colors very effectively. Two other types of flower have also occupied her, *Gaillardia* and *Calibrachoa*. Both have become much more popular lately, very largely due to her efforts.

GLADIOLI

Iva Davenport Austin

Mrs A. H. Austin, 1857–1939, grew and bred gladioli on a very large scale in Ohio. She functioned very effectively in the man's world of flower breeding and commercial nurseries. She wrote a monthly column for *The Monthly Grower*, a journal for gladiolus specialists and was named to the important committees of the gladioli associations. This was a woman who counted. The column was always signed "Mrs A. H. Austin," never Iva Austin.

At first Mrs Austin was just an avid backyard gardener. She did not set out to become a professional nurseryperson but sort of backed into it. Gladioli became her favorite flowers very quickly and she grew them in great abundance. Middle class women did not develop or run businesses in those days but that was what she decided to do. Her husband Amos Austin was a farmer and owned enough land in Ravenna, Ohio, where his family had lived for several generations, for her to expand her interest.

The nursery belonged to both of them but Iva did the crossings. Each year they introduced new hybrids of many different kinds of gladioli. A deep purple one in 1928 was named for Henry Ford. The catalogue shows a grainy black and white photograph of a friend's child, little Evelyn Kirtland, aged about eight, standing next to the yellow gladiolus named for her, *G.* 'Evelyn Kirtland.' The flower was taller than she was.

Iva Austin was very selective with her introductions, only keeping the most effective crosses and taking long enough to ensure that each one would come true after more than one season. All the most prominent breeders in the United

States took her very seriously and shared seed with her. At its peak the Austin nursery sold over one million corms in a year. They handled both wholesale and retail orders. Gladioli were not yet commonplace in most American gardens. It was Mrs Austin who helped create a market for them.

HEUCHERA

Janet Egger

Janet Egger has spent much of her working life in Oregon. She only recently retired from full time flower breeding for a mid-sized nursery. One of her principal contributions has been expanding the range of colors of both foliage and blossom for *Heuchera*, popularly known as coral bells. From being a somewhat modest little plant it has become a star. Doing this takes imagination of a high order. Any breeder must first have an idea of what she wishes to achieve long before coming up with a way to get it done.

Janet started out with a bachelor's degree in botany and then moved to a master's in horticulture. Her first position was with Goldsmith Seeds in California. She wisely apprenticed herself to Mathilde Holtrop there. (See page 199) Following that experience she moved to another firm where she worked on ground covers. After that she joined Terra Nova in Oregon and stayed there for nineteen years as head breeder. Many of her cultivars won prizes and awards. All were patented by her firm. She did not benefit personally. *Podophyllum* 'Spotty Dotty' is another exceptional plant she introduced.

HIBISCUS

ELLEN LEUE

Ellen Leue has just retired from a very distinguished career in flower breeding. Retirement has not stopped her from continuing to develop all sorts of new plants, most notably slightly exotic vegetables with unexpected shapes and colors. Dr Leue is also in demand as a consultant in the seed industry. She has won numerous awards and prizes.

In describing her work it might be simpler to say which flowers she has not worked on. When a colleague told me about her he said he prized her work in hibiscus and impatiens but that was the least of it.

Plant breeding for commerce has five principal sectors: grains, forage, vegetables, fruit and ornamental or flowers. Their importance for world function is clear in this hierarchy. Grains feed the largest majority of the world population. Forage feeds the animals. Vegetables and fruit are vital but not quite so important in the larger scheme of things. Flowers are an elective purchase for beauty, ritual and pleasure, not survival.

After completing her masters degree in genetics Ellen Leue realized she wanted to work in plant breeding. Her path was not smooth. "It was more a matter of prejudice against female breeders in the world of agronomic crop breeding" she says. The University of Wisconsin graduated their first female PhD in Plant Breeding and Plant Genetics. That scholar was Martha Mutschler and she is still a member of the faculty at Cornell University. Ellen goes on, "I stopped for a couple of years with my masters and tried to get a job, but was told by researchers in the field that "MacDonald's is hiring." She did finally land a research job at the NYS Agricultural Experiment Station in Geneva NY, but it was not in plant breeding.

Because she wanted above all else to work in plant breeding she went back to the University of Wisconsin to get a PhD. By that time there were more women in the program, but in general there was a hierarchy of male dominance: "from the most to least male dominated it went 1) Grain crops (corn, wheat, soybeans), 2) Forage (alfalfa mostly), 3) Vegetables, 4) Fruits, 5) Flowers. I didn't know any women at all at the time who were accepted into 1, and just one woman in 2. My graduate work was with potatoes, and I was hired for that at Ball in 1982, assigned to spend 75% of my time on potatoes and 25% on Petunias."

The unit within Ball, PanAmerican Seed, wasn't well set up to handle the potato project, and they decided to shelve it. Ellen Leue took on Impatiens in addition to Petunias, and got more and more into the world of flowers. "When I started, the flower breeding world was really just beginning to professionalize, and many breeders had few courses in breeding or plant genetics, some had none. So it was actually a fantastic opportunity for me. I loved working with flowers, I got to work on more than 20 species over the course of my career - far, far more than I would have had anywhere higher up the "hierarchy" – and I was able to provide some real innovation. It became harder and harder to choose my favorites because they were all so different, beautiful and interesting."

Dr Leue shared this list of her accomplishments with me:

Angelonia, Antirrhinum, Aquilegia, Eggplant, Eustoma (lisianthus), *Heuchera*, Hibiscus, Impatiens, Ornamental

Pepper, Edible Pepper, Pentas, Plumbago, Petunia, Salvia, Tomato, Veronica.

IRIS

GRACE STURTEVANT

Grace Sturtevant, 1865–1947, was the daughter of E. L. Sturtevant, director of the New York State Agricultural Experiment Station. Her father is largely remembered for his classic monograph, *Edible Plants of the World*, and many other valuable books. His influence on his children was profound.[139] Grace was gifted artistically and prepared some of the illustrations for his work.

She was twelve when her mother died but did not resent her father marrying the mother's sister. In fact her young half brother Robert was closer to her than her other siblings. Robert became a landscape architect and developed a deep interest in irises. After their father's death in 1898 the two siblings bought property in Massachusetts. In 1910 they began hybridizing irises seriously, using plants imported from Europe. By 1912 Grace's first hybrids flowered.

Within a few years the iris farm became a local fixture. Grace entered three of her hybrids, 'B. Y. Morison,' a lavender flower named in honor of the director of the National Arboretum, Benjamin Yeo Morison (himself an expert on azaleas) and two yellow ones, 'Afterglow' and 'Shekinah' in the Massachusetts Horticultural Society competitions and won gold medals for all three. She opened a commercial nursery nearby and from that time on the Sturtevant iris farm was considered to be among the very best.

Grace Sturtevant had some very down to earth idea about what constituted the best irises. The plants that survived best in the average garden were superior to her than those pampered darlings on the show bench. She believed that the vast amount of information being gathered by the many individuals breeding irises should be collected together in one place and thus be much more useful to everyone. This insight came to her very early. Grace Sturtevant was a founding member of the American Iris Society in the 1920s. One of her major accomplishments was pursuing improved yellow irises at a time when this color was not found very frequently.

Like everyone else involved in plant breeding Grace Sturtevant had very rigorous standards of what was acceptable. That extended to her own introductions. She was quite unusual in notifying retail nurseries from time to time to discard some of her earlier hybrids as they had not lived up to her expectations. She retired from her nursery in 1945 due to poor health and died in 1947.

LILAC

HULDA KLAGER

Hulda Klager, 1864 to 1960, devoted herself to breeding new lilac cultivars in Woodland, Washington. Her inspiration was a book by Luther Burbank which she read in 1905. Flowers and gardening had always absorbed her and she read whatever books she could find. Burbank's book prompted her to visit him in California. Because a farmer's income does not allow for many luxuries she had to save her own lilac seed year after year.

At first she tried to work with apples and dahlias but

very quickly saw that she preferred lilac. Lilac is in the genus *Syringa*. All she had was a modest house and a small amount of land adjoining it. The land was prone to flooding but her husband eventually built sufficient protection around it. The frequent flooding had brought a lot of silt and made the soil fertile, rather like the River Nile.

Mrs Klager taught herself as she went along. She had not been to any school of horticulture or had any particular exposure to professional plant growing. Everything came from within her. She saw clearly defined goals for disease resistance, broader range of color and variations in the size and structure of the flower clusters and florets. After five years of work Hulda Klager introduced fourteen new cultivars of lilac. She used very simple names such as 'True Pink' or 'My Favorite,' a rich purple, as well as the names of her family.

Three cultivars of lilac constituted her fundamental building blocks. Two had been introduced by Victor Lemoine, *Syringa vulgaris* 'Mme. Casimir Périer,' double white from 1884 and *S. vulgaris* 'President Grevy,' double blue and *S. vulgaris* 'Andenken an Ludwig Spath,' a vibrant purple introduced by Spath in 1883. These new types of plant travelled quickly from France to the United States and then all the way to the Pacific Coast.

She was born Hulda Thiel in Germany but immigrated to the United States with her family at the age of two. Her father initially settled in Wisconsin but when she was thirteen they went west to Washington State. She married Frank Klager in 1880 at the age of sixteen. They lived in her family home. When Frank died in 1922 she lost heart but one of her sons kept encouraging her and she picked up her lilac work again. Due to tireless community effort the lilac gardens were rescued from oblivion after Mrs Klager's death and a non-profit society of volunteers maintains them for visitors to enjoy every spring.

MADAME VICTOR LEMOINE

Marie Louise Gomieu, Madame Lemoine, 1834–1905, was from the same village as Victor Lemoine. She was the traditional French housewife, occupied with the household and her three children, two girls and a boy, Emile. Later in his life, when M. Lemoine's eyesight began to fail, he called upon her to do the actual crossing in his lilac experiments. The lilac's pistils are convoluted and hard to reach. To make the cross required a very delicate touch with pollen on a small paintbrush.

They began to do this work in 1870 when the Franco Prussian War was causing starvation and serious destruction in France. Lemoine thought it would take their minds off the tragedy around them. The first year one of his new hybrids set seed there were precisely seven of them. It was enough. There were ultimately several hundred "French lilacs" over the next thirty years. Lemoine was already famous but this success caused his fame to explode internationally. One really besotted American woman named her newborn son "Lemoine" in his honor.[93] Lemoine Bechtold grew up to become an expert in daylilies.

While Mme. Lemoine did the actual pollination, as did later their son Emile, it was still Victor who laid down which plant parents they chose next. The instruments for her work were very simple and easily obtainable: a needle, a water color paint brush, small scissors and a pair of tweezers.

. . .

Isabella Preston

Isabella Preston, 1881–1965, was born in Lancaster in Lancashire but once her parents died and her married sister emigrated to Canada she had to follow. Middle class young women did not live alone at that time. She was one of five children and had grown up very close to her father. He was a successful silversmith who could afford to send his children to excellent schools. The family all worked in the garden together and as Isabella was the youngest she spent the most time following her father around. She picked up the potatoes as he dug them and grew flowers in her own little patch.

Isabella and her sister left England in 1912, thus missing the most dismal aspects of the first world war. She had spent most of her time running the household as the other sisters married and started their own families but she was still able to attend Swanley College for a short time and begin the study of horticulture.

The family settled in Ottawa and Isabella started classes at the Ontario Agricultural College in Guelph. Theoretical learning did not hold her attention. She wanted to be actively working in a garden. Somehow she found her way to W J Crow, a well known breeder of lilies and essentially apprenticed herself to him. When her practical work showed a lacune in her knowledge she was happy to sit in the library and read as much as she needed.

The next step she took was to become a day laborer at the Central Experimental Farm, working at an entry level job just to get a foot in the door. They had not taken women before and were very wary of her. The situation was complicated by the return of veterans of the war looking for work. After two years her supervisor had persuaded the station's leaders that she was indeed quite remarkable. They drew up a unique job description for her which allowed her to be promoted.

The station made a very good investment. Miss Preston was instructed to work on lilac, roses, Siberian iris, flowering crab apple and aquilegias and she delivered in every category. In addition she made significant improvements in garden lilies which were far too tall for the modest gardens most people could afford. After World War Two ended and the United States began to restore relations with Japan a Japanese admiral was invited to tour the country. He was grateful but asked if it was all the same to them, would they mind if he went to Canada instead to see Miss Preston's lilies. The admiral was a lily fancier and had always been one of her admirers.

The goal in many cases was hardiness. Canadian winters with cold, late springs can defeat many plants. Miss Preston first introduced very floriferous dark lilac without much fragrance by crossing two hardy species but later overcame that defect. In keeping with her English background she chose Shakespearean names like 'Ophelia' for some of her cultivars but also recognized the many women who toiled at typewriters in the station's offices, such as 'Norah' and 'Sarah.' She also cannily named one hybrid for her boss William Macoun who had fought so hard for her at the beginning. The popular Macoun apple is named for him.

Being a woman in a man's world was not too much of a burden for her but did lead to one comical situation. The Experimental Station offered consultation services for any citizen who required them. A very strict Trappist monastery on an island in Quebec requested help and had not the faintest idea that the consultant might be a woman. The monks were so rigid that they did not even allow female farm animals on their land. One assumes that if they needed eggs they had to buy them from another farm.

The collective shock and horror as Miss Preston stepped off the ferry must have overwhelmed them. She was a tall and slightly gaunt woman, hardly seductive in any shape or form but that was not the point. The monks are said to have bundled her back on the next ferry leaving the island before she even had a chance to look into their problem. They carefully kept her off their property, chatting politely about unimportant matters. At least one of the accompanying monks retained the power of speech.

When she retired she laid out her garden in Georgetown, New York to mimic the planting grounds of the experimental station. She enjoyed continuing her work at home. Isabella Preston never married but kept closely in touch with her sisters' families and watched them blossom.

MAGNOLIA

EVAMARIA SPERBER

Evamaria Sperber, 1927–2005, established her reputation in a rather short period of time. She was born in a far Eastern province of Germany, in a region which is now Poland. After World War Two she attended university in Berlin, studying botany and graduating with a degree in agriculture. In 1952 she and her husband immigrated to the United States. She very quickly found a position at the Brooklyn Botanical Garden and participated in their magnolia program.

Evamaria Sperber introduced the first yellow magnolias. Magnolias had not previously come in yellow. She worked at the garden from 1953 to 1959. She crossed two species which had not been crossed before, an American magnolia, *M. acuminata* and a Chinese tree, *M. denudata.* The resulting tree, *Magnolia* 'Elizabeth,' created a sensation. She also introduced two other gorgeous magnolia trees, 'Evamaria' and 'Marilyn.' She does not seem to have continued to work in this field after these achievements.

MARIGOLDS

MATILDE HOLTROP

Dr Mathilde Holtrop, now retired, worked for Goldsmith Seeds for twenty eight years. She was involved in numerous aspects of the firm's plant breeding program and required several assistants to carry out all her projects.

Mathilde Holtrop was born in Indonesia to Dutch parents. The family moved back to The Netherlands just before World War II but soon after the war was over they emigrated to Canada. Mathilde then moved to San Diego and has remained in California ever since. She took her doctorate in plant genetics at the University of California at Davis. Shortly after that she started to work for Glenn Goldsmith. Glenn was beginning to breed *Tagetes erecta,* commonly known as the "African marigold," very seriously.

To give some idea of the size and scope of Goldsmith's plant breeding program the firm employed seven plant breeders at one time. Goldsmith himself was always very active in selecting and breeding. Dr Holtrop played an important role in developing the dwarf form of *T. erecta,* 'Antigua,' as well as the 'Inca' series and 'American Perfection.'

One of her first tasks was to develop a short stemmed

fully double *T. erecta* cultivar with a large head. This became the 'Inca' series. It was very successful but Glenn wanted an even richer double flower. Dr Holtrop crossed the 'Inca' seed parent with an F2 derivative of Bodger's 'First Lady.' This led to 'Inca II.'

She also bred a chrysanthemum flowered marigold 'Merrimum,' and anemone flowered *T. patula* marigolds, 'Aurora.' *Tagetes patula* is commonly known as the "French marigold." Dr Holtrop came up with 'Janie Gold,' an award winning flower, named for her employer's wife.

Much of her work in the 1980s was devoted to perfecting 'Inca' seed for machine plugs, the system whereby individual seed containers were each planted with one seed in an industrial setting. This led to a huge expansion in wholesale plant sales while keeping labor costs down. Dr Holtrop has also bred prize winning cultivars of pelargonium, petunia and pansies. (For a more complete list of Dr Holtrop's cultivars, see www.horthistoria.com, "The Marigold in California," Articles section.)

ALICE VONK

Alice Vonk, 1908–1997, enjoyed selecting plants in her garden in Marion County, Iowa, but gave herself no airs nor did she consider herself to be anything other than a farmer's widow in Iowa. Beside the snow white marigolds she bred she also introduced some improved vegetables using the same method.

NARCISSUS

Mrs R. O. Backhouse

Sarah Dodgson Backhouse, 1857–1921, was the wife of Robert Ormston Backhouse, a prominent Quaker banker. In accordance with the custom of the epoch she had no independent identity once she married Mr Backhouse in 1884 so when one of her narcissus cultivars was introduced posthumously it went without saying that her grieving husband called it 'Mrs R. O. Backhouse.' Sarah Backhouse was devoted to creating new cultivars of narcissus and concentrated on finding one which would be known as "pink," though the color is closer to apricot or peach than that which is commonly considered to be pink. In spite of that *N.* 'Mrs R. O. Backhouse' was the first cultivar officially accepted as pink and was a landmark step in the history of narcissus breeding.

The Backhouse family was from County Durham in the north of England. A deep interest in plants and botany seemed to have been handed down from father to son over several generations. Old James Backhouse, 1794–1869, was a devout member of the Society of Friends and founded a bank in Durham. One of his grandsons, William Backhouse, bought the old Telford Nursery in the City of York and developed it into a leading enterprise that lasted until 1955. After the classic firm of Veitch closed down Backhouse took on the mantle as the place for the elite to obtain horticultural services and supplies. This was similar to the reputation which the Rochester, New York firm of Ellwanger and Barry had in the United States at roughly the same period.

Ellen Willmott (see page 141) showed her independence

of her father when she turned twenty one and came into her own money. One of her first actions was to commission Backhouse to build her a rock garden and waterfall at the family estate of Warley Place. Miss Willmott later bred numerous new cultivars of narcissus at Warley Place. She concentrated on the descendants of the triandrus species. Some were successful commercially.

Robert Ormston Backhouse, 1854–1940, a great grandson of James, bred narcissus when he was not competing in archery meets. Sarah was his wife. They had one son, William. She is believed to have bred more than 275 of a total of 578 narcissus cultivars associated with the Backhouse family. The Backhouse cultivars were introduced into commerce and many did very well. Robert and Sarah lived at Sutton Court, Sutton St Nicholas, in Herefordshire.

OSTEOSPERMUM

LINDA LAUGHNER

Linda Laughner worked in developing pelargoniums and osteospermum for PanAmerican Seed but came to plant breeding via a very circuitous route. In her earlier life she taught the piano. Her father was a devoted amateur gardener and she absorbed his interest as she grew up. One of her close friends bred azalea as a hobby. It was not surprising she attended Pennsylvania State University to study horticulture both at the bachelor's and master's level.

One of her teachers, Dick Gregg wote a manual on the cultivation of pelargoniums. She herself submitted a history of the pelargonium for her graduate thesis. PanAmerican Seed set her to work on pelargoniums but she became very interested in osteospermum and dianthus while there. Linda

Laughner says one of her greatest pleasures is to see the cultivars she introduced for sale in a nursery.

PETUNIA

Mrs Theodosia Burr Shepherd

Theodosia Burr Hall, 1845–1906, was the daughter of William Hall, later Chief Justice of Iowa. Judge Hall always took his daughter with him as he made his circuits on horseback and taught her all the correct names of the flowers and plants they saw along the way. In spite of the great and enduring affection between father and daughter she married William Shepherd very impulsively to get away from a dreadful stepmother. The family was remotely connected to Aaron Burr.

The Shepherd family went to Ventura from the Midwest in 1876 while the town was still in its formative stages. To call it "primitive" is perhaps a little insulting but there was not much there yet. Mrs Shepherd's husband William was taken on as editor of the local newspaper. He was a worthy man, well educated but somewhat lacking in social skills and initiative. They were always short of money. The children needed more than just food and schooling but the Shepherds could not afford many additional expenses. Mrs Shepherd decided to offer dried flower arrangements in return for fabric, sheet music or books through the columns of a ladies magazine.

Her arrangements of dried flowers were so beguiling to the other ladies that she began to grow more and more flowers to meet the demand. Eventually her few acres became a large commercial nursery with a catalogue rich in petunias, begonias and succulents. Peter Henderson, the great Scottish nurseryman who dominated New York horticulture at the time, blessed her work very generously.

Mrs Shepherd enjoyed crossing the petunias but was often too busy. She taught one of her neighbors how to do it. In the following season, Mrs Gould presented Mrs Shepherd with twenty plants, each quite different from the other but all in the grandiflora series. Peter Henderson lauded her work and named the flowers 'The Giants of California.' Some of the descendants of this line, the 'Theodosia,' continued to be grown until the 1950s. Henderson's encouragement led Mrs Shepherd to persist and found the packaged flower seed industry in California.

Mrs Shepherd also worked on begonias. Harry Butterfield's useful booklet on the begonia included an impeccable historical background. He attributed two cane-like varieties to Mrs Shepherd: *B.* 'Catalina' (*B. odorata* x *B. fuchsoides*) before 1905, and *B.* 'Marjorie Daw' (*B.coccinea* x *B. glaucophylla*) in the 1880s. Mrs Shepherd also introduced *B.* 'Silver Cloud,' a Rex variety.

Mrs Shepherd died in 1906 but her son in law and former manager, Willard H. Francis and his wife, Myrtle Shepherd Francis, as well as her sister Margaret Oakes continued the retail nursery until 1916. Mrs Francis carried on her mother's hybridizing.

SWEET PEAS

Hilda Hemus

Hilda Hemus, 1874–1954, was a very enterprising woman who seized the opportunities opened up by the enormous popularity of sweet peas at the end of the nineteenth and in the early years of the twentieth centuries.

She was one of six children of a very prosperous farmer in Worcestershire, two boys and four girls. Their father insisted the girls all be properly educated, quite unusual for that era. Hilda was fascinated by science just as the work of Gregor Mendel was being rediscovered.

In 1899 she decided to work with sweet peas, *Lathyrus odoratus*. Her elder sister Mary also took them up. Gradually Hilda expanded her work to become a truly professional seed person, buying additional land adjacent to the farm for her crop. Many of her new cultivars received awards at the major flower shows such as Chelsea in London and Harrogate in Yorkshire. This led to very bad feeling with another of her sisters, Evelyn. Everyone worked very hard in the business but Hilda was the one who got to shake the king's hand when he gave her the prize and generally be fêted for her accomplishments. Evelyn was very resentful, saying she had done most of the work in the fields and was not given any recognition. In the end the sisters stopped speaking to each other and their grandchildren were not even aware that their grandmother had had a sister.

There may have been a core of truth in the accusation. Hilda had tried to sooth her sister by naming one of her most popular cultivars *L*. 'Evelyn Hemus' but she really shouldered the entire responsibility for what became quite a big business. She hired men to work and employed teams of horses and drays. Hilda did all the marketing and promotion for her seed. One important customer was Samuel Ryder. He had the largest seed business in the country and very cleverly distributed his packages to non-conventional outlets like Woolworths as well as nurseries. He added Hilda's sweet pea seeds at a modest tuppence a packet. Ryder became very rich and relaxed by playing a lot of golf. He used some of his money to endow the famous international Ryder Cup in golf.

An ambitious college student who was interested in Mendel's work used to spend his summer vacations helping on their farm to save a bit of money for the next college year. Old Mr Hemus liked Rowland and allowed him to use a section of his land to grow experimental crops of wheat based on genetic principles. Quite possibly this was part of the inspiration for taking up sweet pea breeding. Rowland Biffen, 1874–1949, became a fellow of Gonville and Caius College at Cambridge in biology and one of England's leading experts on wheat. He was appointed the first professor of agricultural botany at the university.

Hilda was very beautiful and he admired her energy and skill but when he proposed to her she turned him down. She had too much to do and was not ready to marry yet. Undaunted he turned to her sister Mary and married her instead. Rowland's father was the head master of a good private school but the family had no money. Becoming part of the Hemus family secured his future. Rowland was later knighted for his contributions and Mary became Lady Biffen. This sign of privilege did not help the wounded egos of her siblings.

Mary Biffen continued to breed sweet peas and submitted one batch to a competition at the Royal Society in 1900. She won the gold medal for Mendelian studies. Hilda finally did marry in 1916, a Major Ashworth in the quarter master corps. This had kept him safe during the worst years of the first world war. Hilda Hemus disappeared. In accordance with the custom of the time she was now Mrs Robert Ashworth. She had to plow up her flowers and plant the fields with wheat and potatoes for the war effort. When all the local men had been conscripted into the services she raised eyebrows by taking advantage of German prisoners of war to work on her farm.

In 1920 the Ashworths emigrated to New Zealand to escape the British climate. They had one daughter and settled on the East coast in Napier. Hilda tried to grow sweet peas there but the summer temperatures were too high for them to be successful. In 1931 Napier was flattened by the Hawkes Bay earthquake with a magnitude of 7.8 on the Richter scale. The Ashworths survived and their daughter Jean continued to live there until her death in 2009 at the age of 94. She had preserved much of her mother's memorabilia so they were handed on to be safely archived. Hilda Ashworth had gone to Upton in 1954 for a visit and died while she was there.

The Hemus farm in Upton-upon-Severn introduced more than a hundred cultivars over the years but most of them disappeared very quickly. This is not surprising. The "half life" of any new cultivar is about two or at most three seasons. None of her sweet peas are known to have survived though at one time her *L.* 'Prince of Orange' was thought to be in cultivation.

Unknown to the Ashworths, Evelyn, now Mrs Fyfe, and her family also emigrated to New Zealand, living in Wellington on the west coast. Her descendants had no idea there were cousins on the other side of the country. It was only when the author (JMT) was looking into the history of the Hemus sweet peas with a colleague in New Zealand, Keith Hammett and an historian in Worcestershire, Simon Wilkinson, that the connection was made.

AUSTRALIAN WOMEN

Judy Horton, a distinguished horticultural author and historian of the Australian plant industry, very kindly told me about a number of women who are actively breeding new cultivars in Australia at the present time. Many of them are working with native plants such as *Banksia,* "flannel flowers" (*Actinotis helianthi*) and *Xerochrysum*: Kate Delaporte, Cathy Offord, Margaret Sedgley, Kerry Bunker and Jan Iredell. Of necessity this can only be a partial list.

Australian women also work in breeding new rose cultivars. I am indebted to Kate Stanley, an officer of the Rose Society of New South Wales, for this information. (See Appendix) Here again one can only draw attention to a small number of women but that does not mean there are not others. The women below established very fine reputations earlier in the twentieth century.

8

GARDENS IN WOMEN'S PAINTING
AND WRITING

Gardens play a very important role in art of all kinds. Symbolic gardens, used to create a mood in a novel or play, may be quite different from any garden seen in reality, even when the author is known to be an avid gardener at home. The same can be said of gardens in paintings. This is true both of men and women artists. One rather fruitless academic pursuit has been to try and identify gender-specific ways of imagining a garden, either in reality or in art. That dog won't hunt. For every instance of something which seemed unique to either male or female, many others appear and confound this effort.

Imagination and its infinite variations are not governed by gender but arise anew in each artist with his or her unique vision. One of the best known of all artists who painted gardens, Claude Monet (1840–1926), combined great horticultural skill with immense artistic skill and a never-ceasing quest to reach the essence of the subject itself.

One observation may hold true and that is women

writers tend to use a garden as part of their fictional narrative's background more frequently than men. Penelope Lively, a distinguished writer and passionate gardener herself, has drawn attention to this phenomenon, at least among Anglophone authors.[122]

She wrote a memoir of her childhood growing up in Cairo during the English administration in the mid-20th century, *Oleander and Jacaranda*.[123] Her father was a civil servant at the time Britain controlled Egypt. They lived on the outskirts of the city and had large grounds surrounding their house. Her mother was a dedicated gardener and strove to create an English garden. Mrs. Lively recalls the beautiful lawn, glorious borders and shady trees but neither oleander nor jacaranda are part of the English flora. I read this book many years ago, long before I began thinking about these matters and my outstanding memory of the work is in fact the garden.

While a very piquant observation this method is not confined solely to women. One thinks of Nathaniel Hawthorne and "Rappaccini's Daughter."[105] Beatrice grows up in a garden full of poisonous plants and her very flesh becomes poisonous too but in general women turn to this trope more often.

"… there was a ruin of a marble fountain in the centre, sculptured with rare art but so woefully shattered that it was impossible to trace the original design from the chaos of the remaining fragments." Hawthorne goes on to say: "All about the pool into which the water subsided grew various plants, that seemed to require a plentiful supply of moisture for the nourishment of gigantic leaves and in some cases, for flowers gorgeously magnificent. There was one shrub in particular, set in a marble vase in the midst of the pool, that bore a profusion of purple blossoms, each of which had the lustre and richness of a gem." This was no commonplace garden.

Lively makes the very important point that for these imaginary gardens to work they have to seem authentic or at least plausible in that the plants described are likely to grow in the conditions chosen by the author. The author herself needs to be a knowledgeable gardener. English writers were also affected by the experience of living in India and other very hot places throughout the empire.

Rumer Godden grew up in India and wrote about it. In *The River* the garden is somewhat menacing with the river running past it.[102] An English family have a five-year-old boy whom they entrust to the care of the Indian nanny, the *ayah*. They give her firm instructions never to leave him alone in the garden because of deadly snakes or the possibility he might drown in the river. Like all five-year-olds, he is curious and enthusiastic. He had seen a snake charmer at the local bazaar and been very impressed.

He goes out to play in the garden and nanny thinks he is safe. It is hot and she has had a heavy lunch. She nods off. Everyone knows that a large cobra has a nest under a big tree in the garden and the child has been warned about it. On this particular afternoon, with no adult around to stop him, the boy wants to try out what he has seen the snake charmer do at the bazaar. They find him lying dead next to the snake.

There are the obvious "garden centric" books which come to mind, such as Frances Hodgson Burnett's *A Secret Garden* or Elizabeth von Arnim's *Elizabeth and Her German Garden*.

Burnett wrote her book for children in the Gothic

manner, but it remains significant for its psychological insight. There are strong hints of Charlotte Bronte in the opening scenes, an orphan child arriving at a remote gloomy old house on the Yorkshire moors. Both her parents had died in a cholera epidemic in India and she was found alone in a big empty house quite by chance. Most of the servants had also died.

She is not pretty nor does she have an attractive manner. No one has any time for her and we laugh at her spoiled petulant behavior because of her upbringing in India with limitless servants. Under this surface, Mary manages to find her own way in spite of almost no affection or tenderness in her life. She evidently has a resilient core. As the action progresses and Mary becomes less self centered the author describes her appearance as improving. By the end of the book she is now an attractive little girl. Even her dull, uninteresting hair glows.

The Yorkshire servants cannot be bothered to change their routines for her benefit. They have received no instructions. Their master, Archibald Craven, Mary's uncle and sole living relative, is abroad and pays no attention to her fate. They push her out into the garden every morning to get her out of their way. No one hires a governess for her.

The garden is very large and quite formal, rather forbidding. The scene is set. Within the confines of the main garden she comes across a locked gate in an overgrown wall. Aided by some rather suspect magic Mary manages somehow to get the gate open. She finds a small neglected garden: the secret garden. This discovery coincided with her discovering that there is another child in the house, a very sad little boy who is her cousin. The servants want to keep them apart but she is robust and determined and spends time with him.

Resurrecting the secret garden provides Mary with a purpose and helps her cousin Colin Craven, heir to the estate, to heal. The gardener's boy, Dickon, helps Mary to restore the secret garden and one day she manages to take Colin out to see it. Stripped of the Victorian sentimentality, the story shows the amazing therapeutic power of a garden.

Burnett was aware of this long before official psychological studies confirmed this observation. One of the best-known scholars in this field just happens to be a woman too, Clare Cooper Marcus.[127] It is not an exaggeration to suggest that she opened up the field herself.

Colin's mother died when he was born and his father never wanted to see him. The doctors thought the boy would inherit the familial scoliosis. They kept him in bed with a spinal support and he was altogether utterly miserable. He made sure that everyone around him was miserable too.

Taking the boy into the secret garden immediately imbued him with a sense of recovery and purpose. The dominant plant in the garden which had survived in the absence of any human care was the rose. As the crocuses and lily of the valley emerged from the neglected soil, parts of the roses showed signs of life.

In Elizabeth von Arnim's *Elizabeth and Her German Garden*, the author also finds refuge in a garden.[74] A gifted young Englishwoman marries a much older German man, a Prussian count with a huge estate in Pomerania but not too much disposable income with which to run it. Because of the political vicissitudes of the past hundred and fifty years, a Pomeranian estate is now in Poland.

The book is said to be a novel but is very largely autobiographical, judging from accounts of the author's life. Von Arnim did go on to write two highly successful novels, both of which have become films: *Mr. Skeffington* and *An Enchanted April.* One of her first cousins was the New Zealand writer, Katherine Mansfield.

An Italian garden played a significant role in *An Enchanted April* but not in the way the garden did in her first book. On her German estate the garden was one of the principal characters, not unlike Egdon Heath in Hardy's *The Return of the Native.*[104]

The estate grounds had been neglected. Only a small area close to the house was still cultivated. Gräfin von Arnim was immediately enchanted by the entire property and devoted herself to creating a large garden in the English style. Being in the garden provided complete spiritual refreshment and neutralized the stifling social convention of life in Berlin. The unnamed narrator presents her story in diary form. Nothing really ever happens during the book but many pages are descriptions of plants either ordered from a catalogue or put into the ground along with the tribulations of getting hidebound elderly gardeners to understand what she prefers to do. From what she writes, she spent almost all her time in the garden, living on salad and only going indoors to sleep.

The tone is coy, most of it being of the "silly me, I know nothing" variety and it quickly becomes wearisome. What is interesting is the list of rose cultivars with their characteristics properly delineated and page after page talking about other garden plants and what happened to them. The reader ends with a strong understanding of just how therapeutic a garden can be.

"My roses have behaved as well on the whole as was to be expected and the 'Vicomtesse Folkestone' and 'Laurette Messimys' have been most beautiful, the latter being quite the loveliest things in the garden, each flower an exquisite loose cluster of coral-pink petals, paling at the base to a yellow white. I have ordered a hundred standard teas for planting next month..." Her husband (technically a character in the book but most likely in reality too) thought the whole endeavor unnecessary and would not give her any money for it. She had to pay for her new plants out of her dress allowance.

In fact, the husband, a Prussian Juncker, was an unreconstructed male chauvinist pig of the very worst kind. She put these words in his mouth and many more of the same kind. She had been concerned about the fate of poor women always being pregnant and therefore not able to get even close to equality of the sexes.

"Quite so, my dear. You have got to the very root of it. Nature, while imposing this very agreeable duty on the woman, weakens her and disables her for any serious competition with man. How can a person who is constantly losing a year of the best part of her life compete with a young man who never loses any time at all. He has the brute force and his last word on any subject could always be his fist." This is hard to read in the twenty first century.

The use of a garden as therapy for an unsatisfactory marriage is echoed in Natasha Solomons' book *House of Gold*, a very lightly veiled saga based on the Rothschilds.[138] A willful young Austrian "Jewish princess" is sent from Vienna to marry her 3rd cousin in England sight unseen just before the First World War. One witty comment near the beginning is where the author notes that this family liked to collect things. The protagonist's brother said, "Greta liked to collect trouble."

Predictably, the marriage falls apart quickly. Greta's very wise mother-in-law tells her not to think about marriage or her stuffy conventional English husband but instead to concentrate on her garden. With that, the mother in law gives her a hundred acres of land to play with, i.e., gardening as marriage counseling.

One unexpected twist is that the fictional heroine finds a woman's school of gardening not far from the estate and engages the best student to design and manage the new grounds. She interviews "Miss Hathaway" and tours the school. One of the first and best known of these schools was at Waterperry near Oxford, owned and directed by Beatrix Havergal. (See page 115) Unfortunately I have not been able to find any Rothschild who may have supported these schools. The episode remains imaginary. Between the two women the new garden is very naturalistic, powered by Greta's rebellion and strongly influenced by William Robinson and Gertrude Jekyll's theories.

Elizabeth Bowen, 1899–1973, a truly distinguished British novelist, made use of flowers and gardens in setting some of her scenes. She was the only child of a Protestant English family whose ancestors had settled in Ireland hundreds of years before. They owned Bowen Court, a substantial property in the remote Irish countryside of County Cork. Even though she did not live there for very long, the classic green lushness of Ireland left its impression. She was sensitive to the significance of growing things but was not able to be much of a practical gardener. She and her husband lived near Oxford and later in a flat in London.

In *The Heat of the Day,* one of the best fictional depictions of life in London during World War Two, Bowen punctuates a sad moment by having fading rose petals fall on some old love letters.[85] When the protagonist visits the home of a man she is seeing, part of her opinion of his mother and sisters is reflected in the description of their exurban garden: "The façade (of the house) was partially draped with virginia creeper, (sic) now blood red. In the fancy shaped flower beds under the windows and round the sweep the eye instinctively sought begonias. One or two beds, it was true, still showed late roses; in the others vegetables of the politer kind packed the curves of crescents and points of stars." To me this all says stodgy and conventional. One question does arise. What is a "polite vegetable?"

The mystery novelist P. D. James also has some detail about a garden in her books which shows a keen insight.[112] In *Original Sin,* one character shares a suburban house with her cousin, a widow who is a very proud gardener. James characterizes the cousin by describing her "very English" garden: "There was a small lawn with a mulberry tree which in spring was surrounded by crocuses, snowdrops and later the bright trumpets of daffodils and narcissi." James goes on to tell how the garden changed with the seasons, the cousin doing all the heavy work herself.

Ngaio Marsh was born in New Zealand but spent the major part of her life in England, becoming very "English." She describes a garden at a remote sheep station in New Zealand not far from Mount Cook.[128] It reflected the character of the woman who owned the property. The garden was laid out in the same meticulous fashion as one in an English country gentleman's estate. Long paths lead to tennis courts. Another path takes you to a kitchen garden. There are lavender borders and poplar hedges and beds with annuals which do not do well in the climate. Nowhere does the author mention the incomparable native flora of New Zealand in its unparalleled glory. It simply did not occur to the character in the book to make use of it. A garden only had to have plants familiar from "home."

Lively quotes a passage from Virginia Woolf's *To The Lighthouse* which attests to Woolf's thorough knowledge of plants.[155] A family which had spent many summers on an island in Scotland ceases going there after the mother dies. Years pass before anyone returns. The old cook who had worked in their kitchen walks sadly around in the garden thinking of those happier days. She was dismayed. "Poppies sowed themselves among the dahlias; the lawn waved with long grass; giant artichokes towered among roses...." There was no need to use the actual words "neglect" and "decay."

Barbara Pym (1913 to 1980) wrote the most English of novels, wryly understated, very observant and never flashy but very powerful in their muted way. She too was a gardener as can be seen in the following passage from *Some Tame Gazelle*:

"Belinda went downstairs and put on her goloshes and an old mackintosh. She decided to put some bulbs in the beds in the front garden and then move round to the back. If people came to the door it was more likely that they would come later, and by then she would be out of sight. She began to plant tulip bulbs in between the wallflower plants. They would make a pretty show in the late spring. She noticed how splendidly the aubretias had done; they were spreading so much that they would soon have to be divided. Belinda remembered when she had put them in as little cuttings. They had had a particularly hard winter that year, so that she had been afraid the frost would kill them. But they had all lived and flourished. How wonderful it was, when one came to think of it, what a lot of hardships plants could stand!" The author then went on to observe that the same could be said of people and their resilience.

CONCLUSION

The book set out to illuminate the various obstacles and opportunities women faced in gardening. Using information normally scattered among different scholarly disciplines and recombining it this adventure suggests that we have found a U-shaped curve, not a straight line throughout history, if we plot women's work in gardens against centuries. Going back to an arbitrarily chosen onset of recognizable Western civilization, roughly the Norman Conquest, women were the custodians of gardens, expected to grow the food and distil the medicines needed for a family's ailments. The majority of the population lived on the land outside towns. Within the towns many houses still had gardens and orchards attached to them. Maintaining the garden was definitely women's work. The only place they were not allowed to work was the orchard. For some reason their presence in an orchard was considered to be bad luck.

This state of affairs lasted for several more centuries until the rediscovery of classical Greek and Roman learning energized male European scholars during the Renaissance. While a magnificent leap forward in knowledge and ideas, it had the unfortunate consequence of removing women from the few places in which they held any power, keepers of "physic." Turning medicine into a profession, men displaced women as healers and even as midwives. The symbiosis between a woman and her garden no longer mattered.

The beauty of flowers never lost its hold over women and even during times when wealthy women's connection to a garden was tenuous, many continued to work their own plots. This was particularly significant in the eighteenth century when conventional garden history leaves women out completely. Susan Bell accumulated primary evidence about this unexpected activity.

The nineteenth century was when the situation became almost topsy turvy in a very short time. In the first part of the epoch all the rules governing women's behavior tightened sharply, keeping women under very tight wraps by placing them on an impossible pedestal. For a middle- or upper-class woman to get her hands dirty in a garden was simply not done.

In the author's opinion the dam broke when intelligent and strong-minded women in England and America came up with the idea that they should be allowed to vote. Only when they could affect their condition through legislative means would they ever be released from this bondage. Married women had massive legal disabilities holding them in subjection. Heiresses were not allowed to keep their dowries or their own children in the event of a separation. Her money was her husband's to gamble away if he chose. Everything belonged to a man.

The American Married Women's Property Act of 1848

was the first major advance in breaking that stranglehold. A similar act was not adopted until 1870 in the United Kingdom. This coincided with the new practice of impoverished English aristocrats marrying American heiresses to restore their family's coffers.

The agitation over the vote leavened much other discussion, allowing women to think about doing things they had previously been prevented from doing. They could study medicine if they chose. They could become professional gardeners or landscape architects or they could simply enjoy working in the garden around their home without being criticized. There was no limit on their ambition. As professional landscape architects or head gardeners the connection between women and gardens came full circle.

APPENDIX: WOMEN ROSE BREEDERS
IN AUSTRALIA

The author is grateful to Kate Stanley, honorary secretary of the The Rose Society of NSW: Upper North Shore & Hills Regional section for taking the trouble to compile the following list of women rose breeders in Australia.

Active Rose Breeding years	Rose Breeder /hybridiser (No. of roses registered) State	Biographical Details	Awards/ Notes	Registered Bred or Discovered Roses (Modern Roses)
	Mrs Frances Newman (WA)	Husband : Charles Lewis William 1858-1940)(Son of C.F. Newman Nursery man SA) HMF Frances died at 80 in 1962.		Husband -pioneer nursery man popularised Rosa fortuneana stock -main understock WA. "She (Frances)was an untiring worker ...in the nursery (WA)...she had helped produce flowers that she learned to exhibit so successfully" A &NZ RA1962 p.130
1932-1939	Mrs Olive R.Fitzhardinge (11)(patent name entered)(Can be found under Mrs H.C.Fitzhardinge)	Born:1881 Died:1956 (75)	Silver Medal'Best Seedling Rose' for 'Warrawee' tbc	'Beatrice Berkeley' 'Captain Bligh'1939 'Governor Phillip'1939 'Kitty Bice'1932 'Lady Edgeworth David' 1939 'Lady Gowrie'1938 'Lubra'1938 'Mrs C.E.Prell'1938 'Prudence'1930 'Sirius'1939 'Warrawee'1935
1955	Mrs Rupert Downes (AKA Doris Downes(1) VIC Aust & NZ Rose Annual 1943 p.91	Born 1890 Died: 1981 (91)	OBE (4th Oct 1918) for work among soldiers'families. Wife of Maj. Gen. Rupert Downes. See 'The Australian Women's Register' for more information on Doris Downes.	'Lady Dallas Brookes'1955 (Discovered) According to HMF registered but not released. 'Doris Downes' 1931 was a rose named after her by Alister Clark.
1960	Miss Marjorie Walker (1)NSW			'Gem'1960
1962	Mrs J. Kelleher (1)			'Pink Vogue'1962
1962	Miss Helen Sunter (1) SA		"There is a warmth and sincerity about garden friends,longing to give and delighted to receive, or to share the pleasures of their garden, large or small" A&NZ RA 1962 p.132	'Jean McGregor-Reid'1962 Discovered.
1966	Mrs N. O'Connell (1) NSW			'Beth' 1966
1968-2008	Mrs Marguerite H. Parkes (6) NSW	Born 1921 88 (2009)		'Jenny Brown'1976 'Lisa Colfax'1976 'Pink Angel'1974 'Sharon Louise'1968 'Starscent'1976 'William's Rose'2009

Year	Name	Birth/Death	Notes	Roses
1969	Mrs Frances Park (1) NSW			'Sweet Charity'1969
1970	Mrs B.Watt (1)			Lyla Barbour'1970 ROSA lists as 'Lyle' HMF NZ? Or Aust?
1973	Mrs M.B.Gatty TAS (1)			'Stephanie' 1973 incorrectly listed as Joseph Gatty in Modern Roses. Joseph Gatty 'By Joe'1990 & 'Vang' 1980 MR.
1974	Mrs J.M.Dingle (1) Vic			'Kay Barnard'1974
1978	Hilary M.Barclay SA (1)			'Dorothea Howard'1985
1979	Mrs Doris Brewer (1)			'Doris Pleasance'1979
1985-1995	Xavier Sister Mary(2) Tas	Born 1910 Died 1995(85)	'Nano Nagel' registration was in the process of being processed on her passing.	'Iced Parfait' 1985 'Nano Nagel' 1997
1985-1997	Myrtle Robertson (2) NSW			'Cousin Essie' 1996 'Miss Rita'
1985	Hiliary M. Barclay SA			'Dorothea Howard' 1985
1988	Connie Ryan(2)WA	Died 2018	ARA 1991; T.A.Stewart Award 1987	'In the Pink'1989 'Song Bird'1979
1989	Lola Porter (1) NSW			'Tudor Rose'c.1989
1989	Franklin(Pete) & Kay Franklin			'Maids of Jubilee'1989 'Heather Leigh' 1989
1991	Mrs B.Watt(1) (Poss. NZ tbc)			'Lyla Barbour'1991
1992	Susan Irvine (2)	Born 1928 Died2019 (91)		'Bleak House' (Registered under Susan Irvine) 'Niree Hunter'
1992	Leslie Stewart (1) Vic			'Annette Elizabeth' 1992
1993	Helen Diprose (1) VIC			'Helen's White Pol'1993
1994	Mrs P.H.Fairweather			'Jillian Louise'1994
1996	Monica Brady (1) NSW			'Reflection'1996
1996	Myrtle Robertson (2) NSW			'Cousin Essie'1996 'Miss Rita'
1996	Barbara Taaffe (1)Note correct spelling			'Betsy Taaffe'1996
1997-2000	Lilia Weatherly(8) Tas	Born 1932?? Died 2012	Prophyl Pty Ltd (nursery)	'Brilliant Pink'1999 'Elaine Frawley"2000 Freycinet' (Under Prophyl) 'Lemon Silk' 'Light Touch'1997 'Margaret Bushby'2000 Pink Iceberg' 'Rod Beechey'
1998-2002	Merryle & Davud Johnson(2) VIC			'Anne Hall'1998 'Peony Blanc'2002
1998	Wendy Mather(1) SA			'Dove Dale'1998 MATCLOVE
1998	Nancy O'Bree(1)		(NB These are 2 separate entries in MR)	'Rose O'Bree' 'Rosee O'Bree'1998

				DISCOVERED ROSE
2000	Dorothy Harris (1)			'Dorothy's Gem '2000
2001-2007	Margaret Jacobs (2)Vic			'Catherine Frances'2001 ' Prudence Elizabeth'2007
2003	Heather Cant(1)NSW			'Gowan Brae' 2005
2005	Sonja J. Townson (1) NSW	Born: Died:	Roses of Fradee Nursery	'Helen Antill' 2005
2008-2020	John C.& Sylvia E. Gray(26) Qld		Owners Brindabella Country Gardens Nursery	1.Belinda Moss Rose'2019 2.Brindabella Alpha Tiger' 2018 3.Brindabella Blaze' BRONZE MEDAL Rose Trial Garden 2008 4.Brindabella Burgundy Tiger'2018 5.Brindabella Carpet' 2015 6.Brindabella Delta Tiger'2020 7.Brindabella Evered'2020 8.Brindabella Flame'2017 9.Brindabella Flare' 2017 10.Brindabella's Grand Tiger'2020 11.Brindabella Jewel'2016 12.Brindabella Joy' 2020 13.Brindabella Lady'2016 14.Brindabella Monarch' 2020 15.Brindabella Osiria'2017 16.Brindabella Pastel Tiger'2018 17.Brindabella Pink Bouquet'2015 18.Brindabella Pride'2015 19.Brindabella's Pure Heart'2020 20. 'Brindabella Purity 2020 21.Brindabella Sunray' 2020 22.Brindabella Tuscan' 2016 23.Brindabella Zest'2017 24.Captain James Cook'2018 25.City of Brisbane'2016
2012	Mark & Mandy Creed (1) SA			'Barossa Chateau'2012 Syn. BARCHAT
2012	Mrs Mary Frick(5)SA		ARA 2017	FRIsingyel 2018 FRIclisablu 2018 FRINATPARTY 'Saint Angelo View' 2012 FRISTRAVENPIN Syn.'Lacy Parasol'2012 FRIMAR Syn. 'Merlin's Magic' 2012
2012	Pamela Roche(1) Qld			'Bon Bon'2012 ROCHBON
2014	Dianne Durston(1)			'Di's St Mary's' 2014
2015	Brenda Burton (1)SA			'Corey James' 2015
2015	Dianne Durston(1)WA			'Di's St. Mary's' 2014 Syn. St. Mary's Rose

2015-2020	Ruth Walsh (AKA Ruth Griffiths) WALSH Roses		Richard Walsh of WALSH ROSES is Ruth's husband but the attached roses can be attributed specifically to Ruth.	'WALone Syn. Jazz Waltz 2015 WALpassion Syn. Rising Passion2016 Walsatin Syn. Red Silk 2016 WALstar Syn. Star Rising 2016 WALtroy Syn. Troy 2016 Cert of Merit 2018 Nat Trial Grounds WALtrix Syn. Sebastian 2016 WALremmy Syn. Custard Cream Cert of Merit Nat Trial Ground 2018-20 WALclass Syn. Class 2016 WALly Syn. Miss Wallace 2016 WALom Syn. Little Bushfire 2016 WALtrent Syn. Trent, Black Tie' 2017 WALfigured Syn. Hot Red 2017 Walrazz Syn. Coral Sparks 2017 WALnic Syn. Tiny Pearls 2017 WALtut Syn. Gold Tut 2017 WALaud Syn. Audrey 2018 WALbushshine Syn. Bushshine 2018 WALjames 2018 WALloy Syn. Lemon Lace 2018 WALtwo Syn. Barbie Girl2018 WALbliss Syn. Bliss 2018 WALjill Syn. Blushing Barbara 2018 WALjen Syn. Jenny 2018 WALjarrod Syn. Joy Delight 2018 WALgirlfriend Syn. Little Friend 2018 WALjoy Syn. Little Rae of Sunshine 2018 WALrob Syn. Robyn 2018 WALgreen Syn. Green E Rose 2019 WALfire Syn.Fire Baby 2019 WALflight Syn. First Light 2019
2020	Laurel Sommerfield (4)Qld			'Kylie Ruth'2020 'Scout's Rose'2019 'You Are My Sunshine'2019 'Summerfield'
MR =Modern Roses Database for Registration HMF =Help Me Find Database A& NZ RA= Australian & New Zealand Rose Annual				

ACKNOWLEDGMENTS

Professor Peter Stansky of Stanford University asked me to complete Susan Groag Bell's outline. This could not have been accomplished without his constant encouragement and useful comments. I am grateful to him for this opportunity.

Susan Bell's heirs, Yvonne and Robert Bell, have been very gracious in permitting her work to be used. Dr Laura Mayhall is her literary executor and gave me every assistance.

REFERENCES

SUSAN GROAG BELL'S NOTES AND REFERENCES

1. Julia S. Berrall, *The Garden* (New York The Viking Press, 1966).

2. Miles Hadfield, *Gardening in Britain,* (London: Hutchinson, 1960).

3. John Dixon Hunt and Peter Willis, eds.: *The Genius of the Place: The English Landscape Garden 1620–1820,* (London: Paul Elek, 1975).

4. John Dixon Hunt, *The Figure in the Landscape, Poetry, Painting and Gardening during the Eighteenth Century* (Baltimore: Johns Hopkins University Press, 1977).

5. Christopher Hussey, *English Gardens and Landscapes, 1700–1750* (London: Country Life, 1967).

6. Edward Hyams, *A History of Gardens and Gardening* (London: J.M. Dent, 1971).

7. Ronald King, *The Quest for Paradise: A History of the World's Gardens* (London: Whittet/Winchward, 1979).

8. Christopher Thacker, *The History of Gardens* (London: Croom Helm, 1979).

9. Joan Bassin, "The English Landscape Garden in the Eighteenth Century: The Cultural Importance of an English Institution," *Albion* 11 No. 1, Spring, 1979.

10. "Castle Howard," in John Dixon Hunt and Peter Willis, eds., *The Genius of the Place*, p. 232.

11. John Addison, *The Spectator,* No. 37, 12 April 1711, in Hunt and Willis, *The Genius of the Place*, p. 141.

12. Christopher Hussey, *English Gardens and Landscapes 1700–1750*, p. 88.

13. John Lawrence (Charles Evelyn) *The Lady's Recreation, 2nd Edition,* 1718.

14. Jasper Goodwill, in *The Ladies Magazine*, London, Vol. 1, July 1750, p. 291.

15. Christopher Morris, ed., *The Journeys of Celia Fiennes* (London, 1947) pp. 348-49.

16. Ibid., p. 349.

17. Robert Halsband ed., *The Complete Letters of Lady Mary Wortley Montagu* (Oxford: Oxford University Press, 1966) Vol. 2, pp. 403-4, July 1748.

18. Ibid., pp. 407-8.

19. *The Letters and Journals of Lady Mary Coke,* (Bath: Kingsmead Reprints, 1970) 4 Vols., Vol. 1, p. 163.

20. Ibid., p. 166.

21. Ibid.

22. Ibid., p. 407.

23. Ibid., p. 129.

24. Ibid., p. 407.

25. William Roberts of Mrs. Hannah More, (London: 1834) 4 Vols. Vol. 2, p. 278. Letter to Mrs. Boscawen.

26. Huntington Library MSS, MO 4000. Letter to Elizabeth Montagu. (SGB indebted to Sylvia Myers for this reference).

27. G. H. Bell, ed., *The Hamwood Papers of the Ladies of Llangollen and Caroline Hamilton,* (London: 1930) p.198. From Lady Eleanor's "Journal," April 20, 1789.

28., p. 204, May 7, 1789.

29. Ibid., p. 382.

30. Mary Moorman, ed., *Journals of Dorothy Wordsworth*, (Oxford: 1971) p. 119.

31. Ibid., p. 23.

32. *Sotheby's Sales Catalogue of Manuscripts*, London, 19th/20th July, 1976, p. 81. Item 400.

33. On Furber's Twelve Months of Flowers, see Blanche Henrey, *British Botanical and Horticultural Literature Before 1800*, vol. 2, (Oxford: Oxford University Press, 1975), pp. 343-47, and Plates 21 and 1.

34. The Drake-Brockman estate at Beachborough House, Kent, ca. 1745, attributed to Joseph Highmore, in the National Gallery of Victoria, Melbourne. Reproduced in Mark Girouard, *Life in the English Country House* (Yale University Press, New Haven and London: 1978), Plate 128, Color Plate XIX.

35. John Harris, "The Flower Garden, 1730–1830," in John Harris, ed., *The Garden* (London: 1979) pp 40-46.

36. Katherine C. Balderston ed., *Thraliana* (Oxford: Clarendon Press, 1951) Vol. 1, p. 428.

37. Ibid., p. 188.

38. Alicia Amherst, *A History of Gardening in England* (London: 1895); Marie Luise Gotheim, *A History of Garden Art*, Transl. from the German by Mrs. Archer Hind, Volume II, (London: J.M.Dent, 1928) p. 340.

39. Huntington Library MSS. MO 3569 (SGB owed this reference to Sylvia Myers).

40. *The Letters and Journals of Lady Mary Coke*, Vol.1, p. 159, November 24, 1767.

41. Ibid., p. 230.

42. Ann B. Shteir, "'With Bliss Botanic': Women and Plant Sexuality." Paper presented at Eleventh Meeting of the American Society for Eighteenth Century Studies, San Francisco, April 10, 1980.

43. *The Letters and Journals of Lady Mary Coke*, Vol. 1, pp. 167-8.

44. G. H. Bell, *The Hamwood Papers*, p. 86.

45. Robert Halsband, *Complete Letters of Lady Mary Wortley Montagu, Vol. 2*, p. 404.

46. Montagu Pennington, ed., *Letters of Elizabeth Carter to Elizabeth Montagu*, (London: 1817) 3 Vols., Vol. 3, p. 190.

47. Jael Henrietta Pye, *A Peep into the Principal Seats and Gardens in and about Twickenham by a Lady of Distinction*, (London: 1775), Introduction.

48. Alexander Pope, "Ode on Solitude," *Minor Verse, 1700–1717.*

49. Margaret Cavendish, Duchess of Newcastle, "Sociable Letters, Letter XCIII, in Joan Goulianos, *By A Woman Writt,* Penguin Books, 1974, p. 65.

50. Judith Colton, "Merlin's Cave and Queen Caroline: Garden Art as Political Propaganda," *Eighteenth Century Studies,* 10, No. 1, Fall, 1976.

51. Louisa Stuart, *Introduction to The Letters and Journals of Lady Mary Coke, Vol. 1,* p.60.

52. Robert Halsband, *Complete Letters of Lady Mary Wortley Montagu, Vol. 2,* pp. 407-8.
53. Robert Herrick, cited in Elizabeth Kent, *Flora Domestica or the Portable Flower-Garden with Directions for the Treatment of Plants in Pots;* and *Illustrations from the Works of the Poets,* (London: 1825) p. 438.

54. Sir Anthony Fitzherbet, *A New Tracte or treatyse most profytable for All Husbandmen,* (1523).

55. Thomas Tusser, *Five Hundred points of good husbandry,* (1577).

56. Mary Wollstoncraft, *A Vindication of the Rights of Woman,* The Morton Library, New York, 1967, p. 125.

57. Maria Elizabeth Jackson, *Sketches of the Physiology of Vegetable Life,* London, 1811, p. 1.

58. Elizabeth Kent, *Flora Domestica, or the Portable Flower Garden,* 1823.

59. On Jane Loudon, see Bea Howe, *Lady with Green Fingers,* Country Life, Ltd., 1961, and Dawn MacLeod, *The Gardener's London,* London, Duckworth, 1972.

60. Louisa Johnson, *Every Lady Her Own Flower Gardener,* W. Kent. London 1840.

61. J.A.V. Chapple and Arthur Pollard, eds., *The Letters of Mrs. Gaskell,* Manchester and Harvard University Press, 1966, Letter No. 70.

62. *Herbs and Other Medicinal Plants,* Orbis Books, London, 1972.

63. John Lust, *The Herb Book,* Bantam Books, 1974.

64. On the latest point of view of Trotula, see Susan Mosher Stuard, "Dame Trot," *Signs,* Vol. 1, No. 2, Winter 1975, pp. 537-542.

65. Elizabeth Mason Hohl, *The Diseases of Women by Trotula of Salerno,* Ward Ritchie Press, Los Angeles, 1940, p. 9 .

66. Hildegard von Bingen, *Causae et Curae;* German translation by Hugo Schultz, *Ursachen un Behandlungen der Krankheiten,* Ulm, Donau Verlag, 1955, p. 283.

67. The British Museum Catalogue cites four editions of Elizabeth Blackwell's *A Curious Herbal,* 1737, published by

Samuel Harding, London; 1739, published by L.P. John Nourse, London; 1782, Published by L.P.C. Nourse (A reissue); and the 1757 *Herbarium Blackwellian* in Latin and German by Trew of Nürnberg. Biographical information on Blackwell can be found in *Gentleman's Magazine,* Vol. XVII; James Bruce, *Eminent Men of Aberdeen,* 1843, p. 307; Thea Holme, *Chelsea,* Hamish Hamilton, London, 1972, pp. 110-111; Alan G. Thomas, *Great Books and Book Collectors,* Weidenfeld and Nicolson, 1975, pp. 140-1.

68. *The Original Water Color Paintings by John James Audobon for the Birds of America,* American Heritage Publishing Co. Inc. N.Y., 1966, References under Maria Martin; See also, Alice Ford, *Audobon's Butterflies and Moths and Other Studies,* Thomas Y. Crowell Co. N.Y., 1952; and Buckner Hollingsworth, *Her Garden was Her Delight,* pp. 54-67.

69. Elizabeth Kent, *Sylvan Sketches; or, A Companion to the Park and the Shrubbery,* London, 1825.

70. Mary Howitt, *An Autobiography,* Houghton Mifflin and Co. Boston and New York, 1889 (Reprint, AMS, New York, 1973), Vol. 1., p. 263.

71. Louisa Yeomans King (Mrs. Francis), *The Well Considered Garden,* (Introduction by Gertrude Jekyll), Charles Schribners Sons, 1915.

72. Frances Wolseley, *Gardening for Women,* London 1908, Cassell and Co., Ltd., Describes among others, the Thatcham Fruit and Flower Farm School, p. 117; The

Glynde School for Lady Gardeners, p. 119; The Horticultural College Swanley, p. 127; The Studley Horticultural College, p. 136; The Practical Gardening School for Ladies (Regents Park), p. 141; The Edinburgh School of Gardening for Women, p. 144.

73. May Sarton, *Journal of a Solitude*, New York, 1973.

GENERAL REFERENCES

74. von Arnim, Elizabeth, 2018. *Elizabeth and Her German Garden*. United States: 12th Media Services.

75. Austen, Jane. 1903. *Emma*. Boston: Little, Brown, and Company.

76. Austen, Jane (2003). *Pride and Prejudice / Jane Austen: Jane Austen* (Bantam classic ed.). New York: Bantam.

77. Austen, Jane, and Peter Conrad. 2000. *Sense and Sensibility*. London: David Campbell Publishers.

78. von Baeyer, Edwinna. 1987. "The Horticultural Odyssey of Isabella Preston." *Canadian Horticultural History* 1, no. 3, 125 to 175.

79. Baxby, Derrick. 1999. "Edward Jenner's Inquiry: A Tricentenary Analysis." *Vaccine* 17 (4). Pp. 301-307.

80. Bell, Gertrude Lowthian. 1907. *The Desert and the Sown*. New York: Dutton.

81. Bell, Susan Groag. 1982. "Medieval Women Book Owners: arbiters of lay piety and ambassadors of culture." *Signs: Journal of Women in Culture and Society* 7, no. 4 (1982): 742–68.

82. Boccaccio, Giovanni, 1983. *The Decameron*. New York: Norton.

83. Boccaccio, Giovanni, and Guido A. Guarino. (1374) 2011. *On Famous Women*. New York: Italica Press.

84. Boswell, James, reissue 1953 ed. R. W. Chapman. *Life of Johnson*. London: Oxford University Press.

85. Bowen, Elizabeth. 2007. *The Heat of the Day*. New York, NY: Random House.

86. Branca, Patricia. 2014. *Silent Sisterhood: middle-class women in the Victorian home*. London: Routledge.

87. Brontë, Anne. 1969. *The Tenant of Wildfell Hall*. London: Zodiac Press.

88. *Brown, Jane. 1995. Beatrix: The Gardening Life of Beatrix Farrand, 1872–1959. New York Viking, Penguin Group.*

89. Buchan, Ursula , 2014. *A Green and Pleasant Land: How England's Gardeners Fought the Second World War*. London. Windmill Books.

90. Buchan, Ursula and Anna Pavord, 2007. *Garden People: Valerie Finnis and the Golden Age of Gardening.* London: Thames and Hudson.

91. Castiglione, Baldassarre, conte, 1478-1529. (1976). *The Courtier.* London; New York Penguin Books.

92. Chatto, Beth. 1996. *The Dry Garden.* New York: Sagapress.

93. Cusick, Sharon. "Fifty Years Ago This Year: Reflecting on Offerings in the 1961 Hemerocallis Journals." *American Daylily Society. American Hemerocallis Society.* Accessed February 2021. http://oldsite.daylilies.org/50YearsAgo. html.

94. White, Rachel. 2017, July 13. Roald Dahl's Wonderful Natural World. Retrieved February 2021, from https://www.roalddahl.com.

95. Darbon, Leslie, and Agatha Christie. 2014. *A Murder is Announced.* New York: Samuel French Trade.

96. Dollard, Catherine L. 2009. *The Surplus Woman: Unmarried in Imperial Germany 1871-1918* New York. Oxford: Berghan Books.

97. Elliott, Brent, 1986. *Victorian Gardens.* London: B. T. Batsford.

98. Engels, Friedrich, and Florence Kelley Wischnewetzky. 1892. *The Condition of the Working Class in England in 1844.*

With preface written in 1892 ... Translated by F.K. Wischnewetzky. London: Sonnenschein & Co.

99. Fiala, Father John and Freek Vrugtman re-issued 2008. *Lilacs: A Gardener's Encyclopedia* Portland, Oregon: Timber Press.

100. Fry, Helen. 2012. *The M. Room: Secret Listeners who Bugged the Nazis in WW2.* London: Create Space Independent Publishing Platform.

101. Gaskell, Elizabeth. 2012. *Cranford.* London: Penguin.

102. Godden, Rumer. 2016. *The River.* New York: Open Road Integrated Media. https://search.ebscohost.com/login.aspx?direct=true&scope=site&db=nlebk&db=nlabk&AN=1398233.

103. Hardy, Thomas, 1840–1928. (1991). *Far from the Madding Crowd.* New York: Knopf.

104. Hardy, Thomas. 2020. *The Return of the Native.* London: Vintage Classics.

105. Hawthorne, Nathaniel, and Alfred Kazin. 1993. *Selected Short Stories of Nathaniel Hawthorne.* New York: Fawcett Books.

106. Henry, O., pseud. William Sidney Porter, 1907, reissued 1979. "The Last Leaf." *The Trimmed Lamp and Other Stories.* Jamestown Publishing.

107. Hibbard, Bryan N. 2000. *The Obstetrician's Armamentarium: Historical Obstetrical Instruments and their History.* San Francisco, California: Norman Publishing.

108. Hobhouse, Penelope, and Erica Hunningher. 2009. *The Gardens of Persia.* Carlsbad, Calif: Kales.

109. Holmes, Katie. "Fertile Ground: Women and Horticulture." *Australian Garden History*, vol. 10, no. 6, May/June 1999, pp. 6–7.

110. Horwood, Catherine. 2010. *Gardening Women: Their Stories From 1600 to the Present.* London: Virago Press.

111. Hyams, Edward. 1966. *The English Garden.* New York: Harry N. Abrams Inc.

112. James, P. D. 2019. *Original Sin.* London: Faber and Faber.

113. Jewett, Sarah Orne. 2019. *The Country of the Pointed Firs.* La Vergne: Neeland Media LLC. https://public. ebookcentral.proquest.com/choice/publicfullrecord.aspx? p=5703696.

114. Klinghoffer, Judith Apter and Lois Elkis. 1992. "'The Petticoat Electors': Women's Suffrage in New Jersey, 1776–1807." *Journal of the Early Republic* 12/2 (Summer 1992): p. 159-93.

115. Lawrence, D. H. 1987. *Three novellas: The Ladybird; The Fox; The Captain's Doll.* Harmondsworth: Penguin Books.

116. Lear, Linda, 2007. *Beatrix Potter: A Life in Nature*. New York: St Martin's Press.

117. Lees-Milne, Alvilde and Rosemary Verey. 1980. *The Englishwoman's Garden*. London: Chatto & Windus.

118. Lees-Milne, Alvilde and Rosemary Verey. 1988. *The New Englishwoman's Garden*. Topsfield, Massachusetts: Salem House Publishers.

119. Leighton, Ann, 1970. *Early American Gardens "For Meate or Medicine"*. Boston, Massachusetts: Houghton, Mifflin.

120. Leighton, Ann, 1976. *American Gardens in the Eighteenth Century for "Use or Delight"*. Boston, Massachusetts. Houghton, Mifflin.

121. Leighton, Ann, 1987. *American Gardens of the Nineteenth Century "For Comfort and Affluence"*. Amherst, Massachusetts: University of Massachusetts Press.

122. Lively, Penelope. 2017. *Life in the Garden*. London: Fig Tree Press (Random House Penguin).

123. Lively, Penelope. 1995. *Oleander and Jacaranda*. New York: Harper Collins.

124. Linnaeus, Carl. 1957. *Species plantarum*. London: Ray Society.

125. Loudon (Webb), Jane. 1828. *The Mummy! A tale of the twenty-second century* Vol. 1-3. London: Colburn.

126. Mackey, Laura. 1994. *Math in the Garden*. Monterey, California: Evan-Moor Educational Publishers.

127. Marcus, Claire Cooper and Naomi Sachs. 2013. *Therapeutic Landscapes*. New York: Wiley.

128. Marsh, Ngaio. 2011. *Died in the Wool*. New York: Harper Collins.

129. McKelvey, Susan Delano. re-issued 1991 *Botanical exploration of the trans-Mississippi west, 1790–1850*. Corvallis, Oregon: Oregon State University Press.

130. McKelvey, Susan Delano. 1928. *The Lilac a Monograph*. New York, Macmillan Pub.

131. Mendel, Abbe Gregor. 1866. "Versuche uber Pflanzenhybriden." Verhandlungen Naturforschenden Vereines in Brünn, volume 4. pp 30-47.

132. Meredith, Anne. 2011. "Horticultural Education in England, 1900–1940: middle class women and private gardening schools." *Garden History*, 31(1), 67-79. Accessed February 2021. doi:10.2307/1587402.

133. Paige, Judith W. and Elise L. Smith, 2011. *Women, Literature and the Domesticated Landscape: England's Disciples of Flora*. Cambridge: Cambridge University Press.

134. Pym, Barbara. 1950 (reissued 2009). *Some Tame Gazelle*. London: Virago Press.

135. Scott, Walter. 1892. *Waverley*. London and Edinburgh: Adam and Charles Black.

136. Shakespeare, W., Bowdler, T., & Bowdler, H. M. 1807. *The Family Shakespeare*. London: J. Hatchard.

137. Short, Andrew. 2017. *The French Gardening Craze, 1908-1914: Horticulture, politics and the media in Edwardian Britain.* Institute of Historical Research MA Garden & Landscape History Submitted for module 3. Student number: 1444042 https://sas-space.sas.ac.uk/6876/3/ FrenchGardeningCraze_AndrewShort_2017%282%29.pdf.

138. Solomons, Natasha. 2019. *House of Gold*. Random House, UK.

139. Sturtevant, E.L. 1972. *Edible Plants of the World*. Dover Publications.

140. Swift, Katherine. 2014. *The Morville Hours*. London: Bloomsbury Publishing.

141. Taylor, Kristina A. 2015. *Women Garden Designers: 1900 to the Present*. Woodbridge, Suffolk: Garden Art Press for the Antique Collectors Club.

142. Taylor, Judith M. 2014. *Visions of Loveliness: Great Flower Breeders of the Past*. Athens, Ohio: Ohio University Press.

143. Temple, William. 1908. *Upon the Gardens of Epicurus: and other 17th century garden essays*. London: Chatto and Windus.

144. Thaxter, Celia Laighton, 1904, reprinted n.d. *An Island Garden*. Bedford, Massachusetts: Applewood Press.

145. Celia Thaxter's Garden. 2018, January 09. Retrieved February 2021, from https://www.shoalsmarinelaboratory.org/celia-thaxters-garden.

146. Throne, Alice Comish. 1985. *Invisible and Visible Women in Land Grant Colleges*. Logan, Utah: Utah State University.

147. Tolstoy, Leo, and Rosemary Edmonds. 2009. *Anna Karenina*. London: Penguin.

148. Valder, Peter. 1994. *The Garden Plants of China*. Portland, Oregon: Timber Press.

149. Way, Twigs 2006. *Virgins, Weeders and Queens: A History of Women in the Garden/* Stroud, Gloucestershire: Sutton Publishing.

150. Whitman, Louise Bodger. 1981. *The House of Bodger*. Glendale, California. Published by the author.

151. Willmott, E. A., and Alfred Parsons. 1991. *The Genus Rosa*. Sebastopol, Calif: Marion McKinsey.

152. Withering, William. 1785. *An Account of the Foxglove and Some of its Medical Uses*. Birmingham: Swinny, M.

153. Woolf, Virginia, and Michael Cunningham. 2021. *Mrs. Dalloway*. New York: Vintage Books.

154. Woolf, Virginia, 1960. *Orlando, a Biography*. London: Hogarth Press.

155. Woolf, Virginia. 1970. *To the Lighthouse*. [Harmondsworth]: Penguin.

INDEX

ABOUT JUDITH MUNDLAK TAYLOR

Judith M. Taylor MD is a graduate of Somerville College, Oxford and the Oxford University Medical School. She moved to the United States in 1959 and became a board certified neurologist. She practiced neurology in New York and then retired to San Francisco with her husband, Irvin S. Taylor MD. Since retiring she has turned to the practice of history without a license and has written six books on horticultural history as well as numerous articles and book reviews on the same subject.

Dr Taylor was the honorary librarian of the San Francisco Garden Club and reviewed one of its library books each month in the club's "Garden Gazette". Her books include *The Olive in California: history of an immigrant tree* (2000), *Tangible Memories: Californians and their gardens 1800-1950* (2003), *The Global Migrations of Ornamental Plants: how the world got into your garden* (2009), *Visions of Loveliness: the work of forgotten flower breeders* (2014), *An Abundance of Flowers: more great flower breeders of the past* (2018) and *A Five Year Plan for Geraniums: growing flowers commercially in East Germany 1946-1989* (2019).

Women and Gardens: Obstacles and Opportunities for Women Gardeners Throughout History is her seventh book.

Dr Taylor's web site is: www.horthistoria.com

ABOUT SUSAN GROAG BELL

(1926–2015)

Susan Groag Bell, 1926–2015, was born into a cultivated Jewish family in the German speaking part of Czechoslovakia. When the Nazis invaded in 1938 her father sent Susan and her mother to safety in England. He stayed behind to attend to some business but was rounded up and murdered at Theresienstadt.

After an excellent education in England Susan moved to the United States. At a time when there were no academic courses nor textbooks offered in women's history, Bell compiled images of women's participation in society from artworks and began presenting lectures to present roles women had held in society. In 1971, a year after the first women's studies course was offered in the United States, Bell taught her own class on the subject and prepared a reading guide for the course which would become one of the first textbooks to treat women's history from an academic perspective. She taught and researched for more than four decades as an independent scholar at the Clayman Institute for Gender Research. Posthumously, a conference named in her honor was held at Stanford and a plaque recognizing her contributions to women's history was dedicated by the history department of Stanford University.

Biography condensed from Wikipedia: https://en.wikipedia.org/wiki/Susan_Groag_Bell